T0096910

Star Wars: Knights of the Old Republic

Star Wars: Knights of the Old Republic

Alex Kane

Boss Fight Books
Los Angeles, CA
bossfightbooks.com

ISBN 13: 978-1-940535-21-0
First Printing: 2019

Series Editor: Gabe Durham
Associate Editor: Michael P. Williams
Book Design by Cory Schmitz
Page Design by Christopher Moyer

For Ashleigh and Harrison

CONTENTS

"For over a thousand generations, the Jedi Knights were the guardians of peace and justice in the Old Republic. Before the dark times. Before the Empire."

—Ben Kenobi, *Star Wars*

"We so easily accept what's presented to us as the truth, don't we? Isn't it funny how a memory can feel like a whole different reality? People, places, even sounds and colors can change. Or someone else has changed them."

—DiMA, *Fallout 4: Far Harbor*

AUTHOR'S NOTE

IF YOU'RE FAMILIAR WITH STAR WARS but have yet to play 2003's *Star Wars: Knights of the Old Republic*, you should know it harbors a surprise twist on par with the one in *The Empire Strikes Back*. That's probably the biggest reason why we're still talking about this game, while so many other licensed titles have faded from memory. It not only left a lasting impression but was also the first role-playing video game to let players create their own Jedi hero, build a lightsaber, and learn the ways of the Force. Its worlds are lively and filled with mystery, its cast is richly drawn, and its writing is superb. I've replayed it more times than any RPG before or since.

Even if you're *not* so well-acquainted with Star Wars, you probably already know the highlights. It's a sprawling, episodic myth in the mold of twentieth-century epics like those of Akira Kurosawa and Sergio Leone. It blends the sci-fi sensibilities of 1930s Flash Gordon serials with allegories of real-life conflicts like World War II and the Vietnam War. The series began with a trilogy of films released between 1977 and 1983—*A New Hope*, *The Empire Strikes Back*, and *Return of the Jedi*, canonically numbered as "Episodes" IV, V, and VI. The films themselves were engulfed by an ocean of comics, made-for-television cartoons and movies, novels, tabletop RPGs, toys, and video games that turned Star Wars into a pop-culture juggernaut.

From 1999 to 2005, writer-director George Lucas also put out a *second* trilogy of live-action movies—prequels titled *The Phantom Menace*, *Attack of the Clones*, and *Revenge of the Sith*, comprising Episodes I, II, and III. On October 30, 2012, he sold Lucasfilm Ltd. and the Star Wars franchise to the Walt Disney Company for $4.05 billion, and today there are more new stories being told in his beloved universe than ever. Most of these films and tie-ins explore a timeless struggle between warring religious sects (the Jedi Knights and Lords of the Sith), or between spacefaring imperialists and those who dare oppose them. Seen less epically, these are tales of space wizards and laser swords.

Set four thousand years before the formation of the Empire in *Revenge of the Sith*—Lucas's final space opera—*Knights of the Old Republic* concerns itself with the events of the Jedi Civil War, a.k.a. the Second Sith War. This is the same Old Republic that Obi-Wan Kenobi (Alec Guinness) mentions in the original 1977 movie, albeit with a lot less "peace and justice." Keep in mind, too, that the game's story is part of the Legends continuity—what Lucasfilm used to call the Expanded Universe. Legends comics, tie-in novels, and video games were never canonical texts in Lucas's eyes: They are, and have always been, secondary affairs at best. "Once Anakin Skywalker dies, that's kind of the end of the story," he told an interviewer. "But there's three worlds: There's my world that I made up. There's the licensing world that's the books, the comics, all that kind of stuff—the games—which is their world. And then there's the fans' world."

BioWare's *Knights of the Old Republic*, abbreviated more often than not to *KotOR*, is a work that nearly transcends these boundaries, given how often the game's lore and even its protagonist have been featured in Star Wars media and merchandise. From the very beginning, the project was conceived as part of the larger Expanded Universe. Shortly after the game's release, BioWare cofounder Ray Muzyka was so confident in the game that he told the *Edmonton Journal*, "LucasArts is considering this as part of the Star Wars canon, or part of the storyline." Officially speaking, the Legends continuity may be obsolete, but *KotOR*'s influence is alive and well.

Darth Revan, the enigmatic Sith Lord at the game's center, has become a fixture of Star Wars fandom to a degree rarely seen from noncanonical texts. Conventiongoers and cosplayers the world over can be found donning his (or her) crimson-colored mask. In 2006, an online poll published in *ToyFare* magazine earned him a place in the thirtieth-anniversary toy line. In 2015, following a series of fan's-choice polls, Hasbro announced at San Diego Comic-Con that Revan—alongside runner-up Sabine Wren, from Disney XD's *Star Wars Rebels* television show—would join the Black Series, a line of six-inch action figures boasting fine detail and realism. If you know what to look for, Revan's influence is everywhere, and that includes the so-called "new canon" established by the Disney-era Lucasfilm Story Group. As *KotOR* senior writer Drew Karpyshyn once put it, "Revan always belonged more to the fans than [to] me."

And therein lies the bombshell that made *KotOR* so unique: *You* are Revan. Like many of the great Western RPGs, *KotOR* begins with the creation of the player character. A "player character" is the protagonist as well as the vehicle through which players experience the game world: Lara Croft is the player character in *Tomb Raider*, just as Mario is the player character in *Super Mario Bros.*, and so on. First, you're given an opportunity to name your hero, select their gender, and choose between three possible classes—the Scoundrel, the Scout, and the Soldier. I tend to opt for a male Scout, christening him with a hopelessly campy name like "Kem Juraal," or even something as Skywalkeresque as "Dax Starlighter."

Following the successes of the Ultima series and *The Elder Scrolls III: Morrowind*, developers such as Bethesda, FromSoftware, and BioWare have taken to allowing players as much control as possible over their in-game avatars. Class abilities and skill trees let you approach combat in a way that suits your individual play style, while the choices you make during dialogue and elsewhere can steer the narrative in wildly different directions.

"I think most of them played as the light side first, and then the second pass, a lot of them tried the dark side," Muzyka said in autumn 2003. "It was like you wanted to be Luke Skywalker the first time, then Darth Vader the second time. Some people did a mixture, [but] once you start the dark side, it's just so tempting. I found it was like a metagame in itself just to get all the dark-side points I could. It was like, you wanted to be as dark as you could be and see what all the effects would be on your face. And by the end of the game, it was all gray and full of veins and stuff." He told another interviewer, "We joked internally it's almost like getting two games in one box."

So in *Knights of the Old Republic*, the player character is whomever you want them to be, which makes it a deeply personal experience for players.

But it's the shock of losing control over that character—of finding out this hero you've been inhabiting in your exploits across the Outer Rim is, in fact, a Sith war criminal—that makes *KotOR* such a remarkable game. Turns out, you were once the galaxy's most dreaded warrior, a fallen Jedi twisted by the dark side. Later betrayed by your own apprentice in the midst of battle, you were grievously injured, and the Jedi strike team sent to capture you kept you alive using the power of the Force. (The Force is, after all, a kind of magic.) The Jedi Council then made the bold decision to "wipe away your memories and destroy your very identity," to quote one Republic soldier, in hopes you could be made an ally again. So while you have plenty of say over your name, gender, appearance, and abilities, you have no choice about your own tortured past.

And when you learn of your past life, it comes as quite a surprise. Imagine if, during their fateful duel in *The Empire Strikes Back*, Vader had instead told his son that Luke Skywalker was a false persona, a fabrication meant to hide what he truly was: *a Dark Lord of the Sith*. Plausibility issues aside, it's hard to see that kind of revelation playing well with moviegoers in 1980: Luke's too traditional a hero—too purely good for the backstory to stick. In a video game, though, where the narrative demands of the form so often require a protagonist with no family, zero history, and few motivations outside of the player's own whims? It was a risky, inspired move—one that made perfect sense.

Granted, *KotOR* was far from the first story to pivot on the audience finding out that the good guy maybe *isn't* so good. The unreliable narrator, from Montresor in Edgar Allan Poe's "The Cask of Amontillado" to *The Usual Suspects*'s Keyser Söze, was already a well-worn device by summer 2003, when *KotOR* made its way into the disc drives of 270,000 Xbox consoles in just two weeks. Unlike Montresor or Söze, however, Revan has no clue who he really is. His story has more in common with amnesiac antiheroes like *Fight Club*'s Jack, *Memento*'s Leonard Shelby, or *The Bourne Identity*'s ass-kicking namesake. (Those films were released in 1999, 2000, and '02, respectively.)

"We wanted to do a big twist," lead designer James Ohlen later recalled. "In *Empire Strikes Back*, one of the biggest moments *is* the twist, and we wanted to have a similar moment in *Knights of the Old Republic*, where the player's expectations are all turned on their head. So we had a big brainstorming session on what the twist could be. It had to be a simple twist; it had to be a twist that was personal; it had to be a twist that would change the galaxy."

It certainly did. The Xbox edition of the game hit shelves on July 15, 2003, garnering immediate and wide acclaim for its extraordinary worldbuilding and narrative sophistication. "Put this up there with *Halo*, *Splinter Cell*, and any other Xbox game that kept you up way too late," Aaron Boulding wrote in his IGN review. "The galaxy is yours." *Electronic Gaming Monthly* called it "a masterful role-playing game," adding, "It's enough to make a Star Wars fan swoon with pleasure." *KotOR* went on to earn over 40 industry Game of the Year awards, and took home special accolades for best original character and best writing at the '04 Game Developers Conference in San Jose. *Time* magazine later included it on their 2012 list of the hundred greatest video games ever made, where it shared the honor with masterpieces like *Doom*, *Pac-Man*, and *Super Mario 64*.

This book is the result of on-the-record interviews with many of the key figures involved in *KotOR*'s development. Wherever possible, I have made an effort to corroborate specific anecdotes and details, though anyone who's played the game knows just how faulty memory can be.

GREEN LIGHT

WHEN LUCASARTS HIRED MIKE GALLO in January of 1999, the Star Wars saga was on the verge of seismic change. *The Phantom Menace*, the first new Star Wars film since 1983's *Return of the Jedi*, was months from release, bringing a whole galaxy of licensed merchandise—action figures, comics, Lego sets, Pez dispensers, video games—right along with it. The movie, billed as Episode I of the Star Wars saga, would deal with the time period thirty-two years prior to George Lucas's original 1977 opus, showing the fabled Jedi Knights at the height of their influence. It promised audiences a nine-year-old hot-rodder incarnation of Darth Vader, a fresh-faced Obi-Wan Kenobi, and worlds both new and familiar.

Gallo's first role at LucasArts, the video game studio Lucas had founded in '82 as part of an agreement with Atari, involved finishing the game adaptation of *The Phantom Menace*. As its producer, Gallo guided a team of developers working on the PC version of the 3D action-adventure game and then later led an on-site team tasked with porting it to the Sony PlayStation. The Episode I game launched in North America on the same day as a second *Phantom Menace* tie-in, the fast-paced *Episode I: Racer*, ushering in an age of renewed interest in Star Wars gaming. Unfortunately, critics panned the *Phantom Menace* game.

Earlier efforts like *Shadows of the Empire* and *Jedi Knight: Dark Forces II*, both developed in-house by LucasArts, had shown the enormous potential behind the license. But for the next several years, Star Wars games tended to rely less on narrative and more on design gimmicks, with releases pegged to events like *The Phantom Menace*. The reputation of Star Wars console titles, in particular, suffered accordingly.

"Everybody knew that Star Wars video games should *work*," says Gallo of the industry's optimism for the franchise. But the sudden rise in demand for new Star Wars content had inspired LucasArts to ramp up its output dramatically, yielding mixed results.

As Mary Bihr, one-time Vice President of Global Publishing at LucasArts, put it, "We went from a period of games that were very high-quality to a period where, I think, we lost some of the vision, and we were in sort of a survival mode." The company's solution was simple: Refocus on quality. All they needed then was the right source of inspiration.

Many at LucasArts had an immense love for tabletop role-playing. In 1987, a board game publisher called West End Games had released Star Wars: The Roleplaying Game—think Dungeons & Dragons, but with X-wings and lightsabers—and the game left a profound mark, not only on those who grew up playing it but also on Star Wars itself.

"A number of us internally had been discussing the potential of a big Star Wars [computer] RPG for some time," recalls Haden Blackman, another former LucasArts producer. "As you can imagine, many of us grew up playing pen-and-paper RPGs, including the West End Games Star Wars. And early in my career, a group of us at LucasArts were also obsessively playing *Baldur's Gate*, *Baldur's Gate II*, and *Icewind Dale*. So the discussion around a Star Wars RPG was a recurring topic." Simon Jeffery, LucasArts's president at the time, began reaching out to third-party developers with histories of success. "It became clear," Blackman says, "that all of them rightfully wanted the freedom to tell a big, sweeping story."

Baldur's Gate, a fantasy role-playing game for the PC, had been developed in the late nineties by a Canadian company called BioWare. Founded by a trio of practicing physicians—doctors Ray Muzyka, Augustine Yip, and Greg Zeschuk—the Edmonton, Alberta studio was born out of a mutual passion for comics, computer games, and tabletop RPGs like Dungeons & Dragons. *Baldur's Gate*, BioWare's second game, earned widespread critical acclaim and became the second-highest-grossing PC title of 1998.

"It was a long time ago—if not exactly far, far away—so some of my memory's hazy," says Jeffery, who started at LucasArts the same year *Baldur's Gate* was released. "But I was into *Baldur's Gate*, and was so impressed by what it had done in the RPG market, how it looked and felt. So I really wanted to approach BioWare about a possible collaboration, and Haden [Blackman] and I talked it through with a few others. I didn't know Ray [Muzyka] and Greg [Zeschuk], but I figured out how to get ahold of them, posed the idea, and they asked me to come visit them in Edmonton to chat it through."

Jeffery got on a plane bound for the Great White North and arrived to discover that although he wasn't fond of the cold weather, the team at BioWare seemed like the perfect partner for a large-scale Star Wars RPG. "It was an insanely invigorating day," he says, "and I knew there could be something pretty special about to happen. So the team put some thoughts together, I pitched it to Lucasfilm and Lucas Licensing, then to George [Lucas] and the board, and we eventually got a green light to get it going." These discussions took place in late '99 and early 2000, while pre-production on *Attack of the Clones*—Lucas's sequel to *The Phantom Menace*—was already well underway.

"The genesis of the idea was from Simon [Jeffery], Ray [Muzyka], and Greg [Zeschuk]," Gallo says. "They hashed out some stuff and made a deal, and the goal of everyone—which was supported on the LucasArts side by Simon—was to make the best game they could. And that didn't happen that much back then. I'm sure there's plenty of places where that doesn't happen *now*. There's definitely developers and studios out there that aren't gonna ship a game before it's done, but LucasArts, at the time, really didn't have that luxury. This was a big deal to say, 'Look, this game is gonna be made great, or it's not gonna get made.'"

BioWare had the trust of LucasArts, freedom from the baggage of a movie release, and a shared desire to honor the films and tabletop games they'd loved in their youth. The team was in the right place at the right time, dead set on making something great.

CRACKLE AND HUM

"BACK THEN, WE WERE a much smaller company," says James Ohlen, who served as the project's lead designer at BioWare. "You know how they say that companies change when they reach fifty [employees], and then they change again when they reach a hundred and fifty? I think we were between fifty and a hundred and fifty, so everybody knew everybody." This was not the BioWare of the mid-2010s, with its half dozen subsidiaries scattered across North America. There was a strong sense of camaraderie at the studio. Everyone who worked there loved games, and they'd spend their downtime playing and discussing their favorites. Blizzard's early hits—especially *StarCraft*, *Warcraft II*, and *Warcraft III*—were a frequent topic of conversation.

When it came time to work on *Knights of the Old Republic* for LucasArts, the Canadian developer found itself managing a crisis. The studio's longtime publisher, Interplay, had been in dire financial straits for years, and in September 2001 BioWare filed a lawsuit against the publisher and its parent company for unpaid royalties. Two months later, BioWare—in the midst of development on their licensed Dungeons & Dragons RPG *Neverwinter Nights*—terminated their contract with Interplay. "And Ray [Muzyka] and Greg [Zeschuk], our founders, had to negotiate, essentially, an on-the-fly deal with a new publisher, which was Atari, in order for us to continue to be paid and be able to finish that game and launch it," Ohlen says. Many who'd been working on *KotOR* for the past year had to suddenly shift gears and help *Neverwinter Nights* get finished. A five-year project with a team of more than 75 developers, *Neverwinter* had been an enormous undertaking. BioWare was eager to move on to something new.

"I remember we were trying to figure out what our next big game was going to be when we were starting up *Neverwinter Nights* and finishing off *Baldur's Gate II*. And Ray would come in, and sometimes he'd throw some books on my desk and say, 'Hey, you should read these. This is something we should look at,'" Ohlen says. "Funnily enough, one time—the reason I got into George R. R. Martin's *Game of Thrones* was because Ray had thrown it down on my desk and said, 'Hey, we're negotiating with this guy to potentially make a game.'" Video game history is riddled with what-ifs, however, and no such deal was ever struck. Besides, LucasArts had an even better idea.

"Ray and Greg took us all—the core team—into the boardroom," says John Gallagher, concept-art director on *KotOR*. "There were about thirty of us in the room. And they said, 'Okay, guys. We have two offers on the table, and here they are.' They said, 'One's from Sony,' without really giving any details. Just: 'It's from Sony, and it's an RPG.' It was vague. Then, 'And the other one's Star Wars.' And all the air left the room. We're just like, 'Are you fucking *kidding*? Fucking *Star Wars*? Are you serious right now?' So of course the energy in the room starts to crackle and hum.

"Based on some preliminary discussions, LucasArts had identified category leaders in various video game genres. And they said, 'Well, BioWare's—on the basis of what we've seen and what we've played—doing the best RPGs in the game.' So we all got super excited, and then they said, 'Well, you can't tell anybody. At all. Anyone. Ideally, please don't tell spouses.'" Gallagher drove home that night and told his wife the news right away.

Everyone at the studio spent several days in ecstatic disbelief. This was their chance to give something back to the movie franchise that meant the most in the world to them. "And I realize, of course, it's an enterprise—it's an intellectual property created almost entirely, explicitly, to make money. We *know this*," Gallagher says. "But that doesn't diminish the impact that it originally had on quite a number of us. For a good majority of us in the room, Star Wars was the golden goose."

Despite all the excitement, Ohlen was apprehensive about the project. He'd been the lead designer on *Baldur's Gate* and *Baldur's Gate II*, as well as the yet-unfinished *Neverwinter Nights*, but making a Star Wars RPG presented its own set of problems: What types of tabletop game mechanics could be adapted to fit the source material? How would a mix of blasterfire, high-tech gadgetry, and lightsaber combat work in a dice-based game system? What kind of production values would it take to achieve something that felt truly authentic to the Star Wars universe? "And we had a pretty short timeline," he says. "So, while I was a huge fan of Star Wars, it was also a little bit daunting. It wasn't as easy as, you know, making another fantasy game."

In Dungeons & Dragons and similar tabletop games, players roll physical dice to determine whether or not their actions will be successful—a melee attack, a magical defense spell, a treacherous climb. For the Baldur's Gate series, BioWare had implemented a combat system using virtual dice, which simulated the turn-based flow of D&D skirmishes. As luck would have it, a new tabletop Star Wars RPG was also in development during the conceptual stages of *KotOR*.

"I might have been the first to suggest using the Wizards of the Coast d20 ruleset as the underlying system," says Haden Blackman, "partly because I liked that the other BioWare games were based on the D&D core rules and partly because I was constantly pushing for more collaboration between LucasArts and other Star Wars creators." A lot of Star Wars material crossed his desk early in development during his tenure at LucasArts, so Blackman knew Wizards of the Coast had a new pen-and-paper RPG in the works. He felt the Star Wars Roleplaying Game (2000), built on the same trademarked d20 System that Wizards used for its Dungeons & Dragons products, would be a natural fit for BioWare's Star Wars game.

"We wanted to capture the idea of playing an RPG with your friends—you know, playing an old-school tabletop, D&D-style RPG," says *KotOR* senior writer Drew Karpyshyn. "The big appeal of that is, you're with your friends, there's a lot of interaction. Things *you* do affect what *they* do. Things *they* do affect what *you* do." Except in this case, you'd be interacting with non-player characters, or NPCs. In most BioWare RPGs, two or three AI characters typically follow you wherever you go, fighting alongside you in battle and striking up the occasional conversation.

"Those companion characters, your squadmates, and the way they interact with you really makes you feel like there are other people with you on this journey," Karpyshyn says. "And that's something you can leverage in games in a way you can't in something like a novel. In a novel, you don't get that interaction—you don't get the back-and-forth—whereas in a game you can be more responsive to the player and the audience, so it's really a unique situation."

"The thing that I remember pretty vividly about the beginning of this project was the initial pitch doc that we got from BioWare," says producer Mike Gallo. "Once the discussions were happening, they put together a story pitch and a gameplay pitch, and the very first thing that we talked about doing was a *Baldur's Gate*–style Star Wars game—action-oriented, with RPG elements, and that kind of three-quarter, isometric view. And that's what the initial thinking was. It was gonna be PlayStation *and* Xbox; it wasn't gonna be just an Xbox and PC game. Pretty quickly, it became apparent that that wasn't gonna be the right way to go."

Meanwhile, *Neverwinter Nights* aimed to raise the bar with its rich, full-3D graphics and technical complexity. Because their timelines for *Neverwinter Nights* and *Knights of the Old Republic* overlapped, BioWare knew they'd need to rely on tech like the AI and character-generation tools they'd already built for *Neverwinter* when they got around to making *Knights of the Old Republic*. But *Neverwinter*'s Aurora Engine would also have to evolve in order to support the development of both Xbox and PC versions of the Star Wars game.

In a 2002 interview with GameSpot, Gallo explained that "the engine itself is based on *Neverwinter Nights*'s engine, but it's actually been almost completely rewritten for *Star Wars*." When I spoke to him on the phone in September of 2017, he took the opportunity to further clarify: "With these types of technology—it's very difficult to call something an 'engine' or a 'tool.' Or whatever it is. It is *far* more complex than that. And technically a lot of this stuff is iterative, but they're basically tearing those things down and rebuilding them every time. Making them more efficient, making them perform better, doing whatever they need to do to take advantage of the hardware. So, yes, it was a new engine built on their knowledge and their tech that they had built up with their previous games." The Odyssey Engine, as it became known, would later be used for BioWare's original RPG *Jade Empire* (2005) as well as Obsidian Entertainment's *Knights of the Old Republic II: The Sith Lords* (2004).

"During *Knights of the Old Republic*, that wasn't the only project I was working on [at LucasArts]," Gallo says. "Because they were external projects [involving collaborations with other companies], typically people who were on the production team would have two or three or more projects they were managing. That year was pretty rough because they had asked me to manage the team that was doing *Star Wars: Obi-Wan* when we made the decision to move it from PC to Xbox. And so I was working with a group on the internal team for that, and then also occasionally going up to Edmonton and working with a group from BioWare. A lot of time with the BioWare guys was spent in prototype and design and concept, so a lot of [my] involvement was making sure that approvals were happening."

And the approvals process at LucasArts was extensive. "We were working with the marketing team and licensing department at Lucasfilm and making sure that everything was getting approved through them. At that time, George Lucas was pretty involved in approving that stuff, so we would get notes back from him that we would have to address. We never got to meet with him during that time, but we were still getting notes from him."

It was an incredibly busy time for LucasArts. In addition to *Knights of the Old Republic* and *Obi-Wan*, the publisher also released twelve other Star Wars games in the three-year period from 2001 to 2003: *Star Wars: Starfighter* (Feb. 2001); *Star Wars: Super Bombad Racing* (Apr. 2001); *Star Wars: Galactic Battlegrounds* (Nov. 2001); *Rogue Squadron II: Rogue Leader* (Nov. 2001); *Star Wars: Racer Revenge* (Feb. 2002); *Star Wars: Jedi Starfighter* (Mar. 2002); *Jedi Knight II: Jedi Outcast* (Mar. 2002); *Star Wars: The Clone Wars* (Oct. 2002); *Star Wars: Bounty Hunter* (Nov. 2002); *Jedi Knight: Jedi Academy* (Sept. 2003); *Rogue Squadron III: Rebel Strike* (Oct. 2003); and the massively multiplayer (and massively ambitious) online game *Star Wars Galaxies* (June 2003).

"God bless the guys at BioWare, and Simon Jeffery, and Haden [Blackman]'s contributions," Gallo says.

"Haden and I shared an office for the whole time that *Knights* was in production while he was working on *Star Wars Galaxies*. So there were times where that was the tensest office in the entire building because of what was riding on those two games. And I felt Haden had a much more difficult problem than I did." After all, *Galaxies* was to be the first-ever Star Wars MMO, a shared online sandbox that would require support over the span of nearly a decade.

Knights of the Old Republic, as the first Star Wars role-playing video game, was also a massive gamble. As a console RPG for the Xbox, it had to follow Bethesda's 2002 masterpiece, *The Elder Scrolls III: Morrowind*. It also had to tell an all-new, original story in the Star Wars universe—which would revolve around the player's experiences—yet stay true to the spirit of the source material. Former LucasArts VP Mary Bihr was especially worried about the untested waters of the Old Republic setting. "Maybe archetypes weren't enough," she wondered. "Maybe people wanted to play [as] Han Solo. Maybe they wanted Darth Vader in the game."

Ultimately, LucasArts had faith in BioWare's vision.

"Back then, and even today, being part of *KotOR* was the highlight of my career," Jeffery says. "I was just drawn into this incredible arc that BioWare was developing; Mike Gallo's updates to the team were one of the highlights of the time. Everyone looked forward to seeing how the game was progressing, new characters, and how they fit into the fabric of the Star Wars universe."

Jeffery remembers well the day BioWare suggested scrapping the idea of *KotOR* as an isometric game. "BioWare said that they didn't want to do that. They wanted to do something completely different and make a 3D RPG." To some, this was a case of fixing what wasn't broken. *Neverwinter Nights* was still in development and had not yet proven BioWare's capacity for making quality 3D games, and Baldur's Gate was the studio's claim to fame. That series used a top-down, aerial perspective to create the illusion of three dimensions within a 2D game engine.

"I think what LucasArts envisioned when they signed us was that we were gonna make, essentially, '*Baldur's Gate* in Space,'" Ohlen says. "In fact, I think they complained about the fact we *didn't* make '*Baldur's Gate* in Space.' Because, like usual, we were over budget and behind schedule."

"I had a cow," Jeffery recalls of the team's decision to shift from an isometric viewpoint to full 3D. "It was not at all what I had been imagining. But somehow they—and Mike Gallo—talked me around. Sometimes I love being proven wrong, and they did that spectacularly." Ultimately, the choice to abandon BioWare's signature visual style lent *Knights of the Old Republic* the immersive quality befitting a cinematic Star Wars experience. But to truly capture the spirit of Star Wars, *KotOR* was also going to need a story worth telling.

A MORE CIVILIZED AGE

THE STAR WARS UNIVERSE has no shortage of sequels, prequels, and spinoffs. Even before George Lucas's prequel trilogy debuted in 1999, fans of Star Wars were hungry for details on what happened before, after, and even in between the films that form the narrative center of the franchise. It might have seemed intuitive, then, for LucasArts to develop a tie-in game pegged to the release of 2002's *Attack of the Clones*.

"It has to be said that there were certainly a few people at the time who thought we should have done an RPG set in the *Episode II* time frame, as that was current and likely an easier sell-in to retail," says Simon Jeffery. But this approach posed a significant creative challenge.

"There was a pretty deep understanding that doing a movie tie-in game would just be—not a good thing," lead designer James Ohlen says. "Because our timeline would definitely have to be dictated by the movie, and the kind of stories that we like to tell at BioWare are epic in scope, where the player is the hero who's defeating the big bad—the evil that's threatening the land or the universe or the galaxy. And if it were an *Attack of the Clones* tie-in, the players *would not be* the heroes of the galaxy. That would be Anakin Skywalker and Obi-Wan Kenobi." The marriage of BioWare's *Neverwinter* tech with the Star Wars universe was too great an opportunity to squander on another mediocre, run-of-the-mill movie tie-in.

"We were already working on [the *Galaxies* MMO] set during the Galactic Civil War [seen in Episodes IV, V, and VI], so we wanted to avoid that, too," says Haden Blackman. It was clear the developers needed to look elsewhere for inspiration. "Internally, we also really wanted to focus on the Jedi and the Sith. We knew that Jedi were going to be rare in *Galaxies*, and we wanted a game that gave players that core fantasy." *Galaxies* would take place during the events of the original Star Wars trilogy, at which point the Jedi are thought to be extinct. "And I, personally, wanted to see Jedi and Sith going toe-to-toe. I felt that the best way to both give the developers the space within the existing timeline to really own the story and characters, and allow us to explore a major conflict between the Jedi and the Sith, was to set it in the past—well before the prequels."

Setting the game in a new era would give the writers maximum creative freedom, and would also allow for a nonlinear story in which the player's choices could influence the state of the galaxy without breaking the established continuity. "When you're tied to using Darth Vader and Luke Skywalker and all those characters that everybody knows, there's just certain things that you *cannot do*," Mike Gallo says. "You can't have some of that freedom." The player couldn't, for example, have Luke Skywalker decide to murder an innocent bystander and fall prey to the dark side of the Force. "Those characters already have their arc, so it would've been very difficult to do anything substantial to those characters, because we couldn't tell a story that was after *Return of the Jedi*." BioWare would also be severely limited as to what kinds of surprises they could put into a preexisting narrative. "If we had to tell it *in between* the movies, you have your boundaries determined from the very beginning. Had we gone that way, it would have made it a much more difficult proposition. And it wouldn't have played to the strengths of BioWare. Too much of [the story] would've been predetermined. It would've been like bowling with bumpers: 'You can't stray *too far*.'" In order to tell a mythic, BioWare-caliber story with the player at its center, LucasArts instead suggested setting the game 4,000 years before the events of the films.

"My original hopes and dreams were for a game with the same perspective as *Baldur's Gate* but with badass Old Republic Jedi," Jeffery says. "I remember someone famously said they couldn't imagine 'cavemen Jedi running around with lightsabers.' But one look at the source material was all it took for most people to get it." Still, there was more established writing about the ancient history of the Star Wars universe than a casual fan of the films might realize.

"I remember talking about *Golden Age of the Sith*, and basically passing around those trade paperbacks at the office," Gallo says, referring to one of the earliest comic book depictions of the Old Republic era. "I had read some of those comics back when they'd come out from Dark Horse, but we were kind of resurrecting that stuff and reading through it, and it made a lot of sense. One of the working titles [for *KotOR*], initially, was either *Age of the Sith* or *Tales of the Jedi*—it was directly named after one of those comics."

"I was fascinated by how much some of the folks at LucasArts knew about the Star Wars canon," says Jeffery. "One guy in particular was just this incredible rock star of knowledge: Haden Blackman. He showed me some of the Old Republic comics, and I loved them. He had some ideas about a game set in that era, and I completely fell in love with the concept."

"Fortunately, the Dark Horse comics—which I knew quite well, having worked on an interactive Star Wars encyclopedia for LucasArts [called *Behind the Magic*]—had already opened that door for us," Blackman remembers. "I pitched the idea to Simon and then again to Lucasfilm using that rationale, and we got the go-ahead. I believe Simon then approached BioWare with the high concept, and they took it from there. So BioWare was responsible for the story, the characters, et cetera; my contribution was suggesting the time period and working with Lucasfilm Licensing to get approval to set the game during that era. I also provided a high-level style guide to help BioWare navigate Star Wars. Beyond that, there were a lot of little details, but nothing major—some suggestions on how the Dark Horse comics could be referenced, for example, or some name ideas."

"The decision to do it in that era just opened everything up," Gallo says, "and allowed us to do a ton of things, including the big twist, which we wouldn't have been able to do in the regular universe."

"Truth is, we were taking a massive gamble by doing something completely outside of the LucasArts playbook," Jeffery says. "Once the core group of us at LucasArts decided that we wanted to do this, all of us had the mantra of wanting this to be our dream game."

"My philosophy, when you're the creative lead on a video game or a role-playing game, is that what you're really doing is creating a fantasy fulfillment—especially if you're working with an intellectual property—for *fans of that IP*," Ohlen says. "It's about crafting an experience that the fans of that property are going to love, and so I always go to the source material. One of my strengths—maybe one of my flaws, as well—is that my tastes are very mainstream. My favorite movie is *Empire Strikes Back*. I think the majority of Star Wars fans' favorite movie is *Empire Strikes Back*. I wanted *Knights of the Old Republic* to be as close to the feeling that you got when you watched that movie as possible. And, obviously, the original *Star Wars*. I also loved the space battle at the end of *Return of the Jedi*; I felt that was something fans would want to see. You've gotta have the epic space battle at the end that determines everything while a ground battle is happening simultaneously."

"I think there's two big draws to [the Old Republic] era," Karpyshyn says. "One is that you have *armies* of Jedi and Sith, so you're not restricted to one or two or a handful of characters like in the original movies. So it just makes it easier to have them be part of the story you're telling. The other thing is, there wasn't a lot fleshed out in that era, so we were given more of a blank canvas. With the Old Republic, we got to paint our own universe within the Star Wars setting."

On the second page of an old BioWare pitch document, buried in Gallo's files and unseen for more than a decade, there's a familiar quote: "For over a thousand generations, the Jedi Knights were the guardians of peace and justice in the Old Republic."

Alec Guinness had a lot of great lines in the original Star Wars, but none sparks the imagination quite like

Ben Kenobi's tale of a bygone era and its mythic heroes. At the turn of the millennium, of course, George Lucas began telling his own stories set just before the rise of the Empire—territory that had for years been relegated to licensed tie-in comics and background material. But BioWare and LucasArts saw further potential in the vast history Kenobi's words implied.

"And that was the guiding light at the very beginning of the project: We're gonna tell the story of those guys," Gallo says. "We're gonna dig into that lore—those Knights of the Old Republic."

BINARY SYSTEM

ONCE LUCAS LICENSING APPROVED the game's *Tales of the Jedi*–era setting, the real work commenced. For producer Mike Gallo, that meant keeping an open line of communication between BioWare and the many caretakers of the Star Wars Expanded Universe. It also involved lots of administrative tasks—poring over design docs, story drafts, and production schedules. Not to mention flying up to Edmonton periodically to check on BioWare's progress in person.

"I pretty much had no life outside of work," Gallo recalls with a laugh. "I remember my friends getting mad at me because I had to constantly cancel on them, or just not even accept plans. I'm just like, 'I don't know what to tell you. We're makin' a game!' And back in those days, I didn't even care—I could work twelve or sixteen hours every day and not even think about it."

Gallo had been a Star Wars fan since he was five years old, watching the original *Star Wars* at the drive-in with his father. Some of his earliest memories are of C-3PO stranded on Tatooine, Han Solo and Luke Skywalker infiltrating the Death Star, and Luke taking flight with Red Squadron at the Battle of Yavin. Although he'd fallen in love with games because of the Commodore 64 and titles like Interplay's *Wasteland* (1988), LucasArts was the company responsible for keeping him engaged with the medium, even after he began his career as a tester at Konami of America in 1991.

"I didn't have a computer," he says, "so I'd bring my computer home from work over the weekend, just so I could play LucasArts games like *Indiana Jones and the Fate of Atlantis*, *Day of the Tentacle*, and the X-Wing series."

Seven years after he got his start at Konami, some friends in the industry mentioned that there was a job opening for a producer on the *Phantom Menace* video game adaptation, and Gallo managed to secure an interview.

"Working at LucasArts was *the dream*," he says. "It was a lot of crunch and overtime and firefighting. But I think back to those times and realize how *fun* a lot of it was, and how much work it was, and kind of how terrible of a producer I was back then. The thing that got me through was being able to firefight, being passionate about games and movies and the subject material, and having a basic understanding of a lot of the work that would have to go into getting things fixed. I looked at things very much from a tester point of view, so I was able to understand, through years of doing that—very low-level—how things worked."

Whatever his shortcomings, the team at BioWare loved Gallo's approach.

"We were pretty stubborn back then," says James Ohlen. "Obviously, we had to work heavily with [LucasArts] on the story to make sure that everything we were doing fit within the canon of the Old Republic universe. But the thing about working with LucasArts, I found, was that the partnership with them was a lot easier, and a lot more satisfying, than when we had been working on Dungeons & Dragons titles. LucasArts gave us a lot of autonomy. They allowed us to do our thing, they had a lot of trust in us, and there weren't a lot of egos involved. They didn't say, 'You need to change this because my son didn't like it.' Or, 'You need to change this because *I just don't like it*.' They were very professional. George Lucas had created—and I think this was why Star Wars grew during the 1990s—a culture where creators in the universe had a lot of freedom to explore and add to the Star Wars galaxy the way they wanted to."

"[The team at LucasArts] were mostly in a support role," says Drew Karpyshyn. "They were actually very good about letting us do our own story. Now, of course, they had approvals, and they would give feedback on what they liked or didn't like. But they were willing to step back and let us do our thing, which made it very easy to work with them. So they were very supportive, but they would only come in as we needed various approvals. At BioWare, we were pretty much allowed to work on things in our way, in our own time."

"I just recall both Haden and Mike being really easygoing guys to work with," says concept-art director John Gallagher. "They had to be administrators—or curators and archivists—of ensuring that the integrity of the license was maintained. That it maintained that flavor. And we were all pretty judicious. We didn't want to let Star Wars down. So we were all pretty self-regulating in terms of ensuring that what we were offering was the best that we could in the Star Wars universe. And creating this new [part of that world] was really quite a privilege, so obviously we didn't want to misstep on that, either. But in terms of what I did, it was just a lot of thumbs-up: 'Yeah, kickass, cool, love it, great, awesome.' I remember very little response or feedback that was anything but, 'Outstanding. Keep it up.' I think the art was handled pretty well. The team was pretty full-on A-level, so there were no real concerns about the work not being up to spec."

"It was an incredibly exciting time at LucasArts," says Haden Blackman, "because we did have these two massive projects in development with outside groups. The prequels were in production, but our focus was really on these two new Star Wars experiences, both of which were unlike anything we'd done before. The thing I remember most about BioWare was the unyielding commitment to quality. They worked so hard on the game, and every build felt like a huge leap forward."

But that's not to say it was easy.

"Dungeons & Dragons was very much a pen-and-paper role-playing game with a set of rules that are very tactical in nature, and Star Wars comes from movies with epic battle sequences, so the combat had to feel more cinematic, action-packed, and more like the films," Ohlen explains. "So we had to get away from the more tactics-based combat that you see in *Baldur's Gate*. We didn't want to have the top-down camera, we didn't want to have a big party with so many people to manage, and we didn't want players to have to pause the game and strategize as much as they had in the *Baldur's Gate* series. With *Knights of the Old Republic*, we wanted the combat to flow faster. We wanted to experiment with—and I think we successfully did it—the synchronized lightsaber clashing, which was something that we got from *Neverwinter Nights*. We'd developed some synchronized combat, and we took that and made it a lot better in *Knights of the Old Republic* for the lightsaber combat."

According to Ohlen, so many of these changes came simply from trying to make a game that felt less like D&D and more like Star Wars. "We wanted a lot less reading and a lot more voice-over," he says, "so we went from top-down-camera conversations to the more obviously cinematic conversations. Dungeons & Dragons is all about killing monsters and looting their corpses. So, while we still have loot in *Knights of the Old Republic*, we didn't lean into it as much as we had in the D&D titles, because Star Wars is definitely not about *that*."

"They did a lot of work," Mike Gallo says. "The way that the combat system in that game was built, and the way that the animations were tied together to work, was a pretty complicated undertaking. It was one of the key things that made that game work. Having two characters locked in lightsaber combat, fighting, seems fairly commonplace: That is just something you can do. But the way that it worked in that game—those things were choreographed and animated together. And to tie that stuff together, to get it to look right, the whole point of that was to make it look like the films as much as you could. And you have to be able to do that anywhere in the level, and solve those problems with being able to do that within the combat space, which could be anywhere. Yes, it was turn-based, but you didn't get that *feel* from the way the combat flowed. And that was the whole point of how they were building that combat system and the animations for it: to make it feel like it flowed, and that it wasn't turn-based."

Perhaps the biggest challenge BioWare faced was in making a full-fledged RPG that would still be intuitive for players using the Xbox gamepad, as opposed to a keyboard and mouse. "This was our first console RPG," Ohlen says. "The interface was a difficult challenge when it came to combat because it was built off the *Neverwinter Nights* engine, which was a PC game designed for mouse and keyboard. And we were also doing a party-based system with pause-and-play combat, which had been inspired by *Baldur's Gate*, another mouse-and-keyboard game. That's one area where we were struggling until the very end: 'How do we get the [Xbox] interface to be understandable—to not be clunky?' It wasn't *spectacular*, by any means, but I think we were able to solve it to a point where it wasn't a detractor from people's enjoyment of the game."

The first playable demo BioWare showed the press, at E3 in summer 2001, was very different from the game *KotOR* would become. According to Gallo, it was even built in a different engine. "It was a *vision piece*, basically," Gallo says. "It was, 'This is the vision for this game. This is how we want this thing to look.' I can't remember how much time we spent on that in the demo—how much of it we showed to people. It was probably fifteen to thirty minutes of very slowly walking through this stuff, and showing off the technology, and showing off the art style. And then getting deeper into,

'Hey, now we're gonna show you some more detail on our characters.' Because all of our characters talked, so they all had to have lip sync, and there was all this kind of deep dive into that technology, and the bones and the foundations of everything. It was the BioWare guys—primarily Casey and James—running that demo over and over again for four days of E3."

LucasArts demoed an area of Anchorhead, a settlement on Luke Skywalker's home planet, Tatooine, as well as a small portion of Taris, a new world original to *Knights of the Old Republic*. A reporter for GameSpot noted that the combat between Jedi and Sith "resembled the final fight sequence in Episode I, complete with back flips, twirling sabers, and high kicks." IGN agreed the footage looked "pretty damn nice."

"LucasArts always showed games behind closed doors," says Haden Blackman, "but that year *Galaxies* and *KotOR* shared a demo room that was even more exclusive—invitation-only for a select group of press and retailers. The *Galaxies* demo showed off some of the immersive environments we were trying to create: a swamp on Naboo and part of Tatooine. For *KotOR*, we really focused on the story and characters, with a ton of concept art that hinted at things to come."

"The thing that was awesome about it was how much it looked like the Star Wars universe," Gallo says. "One of the biggest challenges was getting the combat to work, because the characters were gonna be locked [in position]. But there were questions: *Is this gonna take? How is the combat gonna look? How's this gonna feel?* Because it [was turn-based]; you're issuing commands in real time, but it's not immediate action because it's being driven by the d20 System—all that stuff. We saw animation tests, and all that stuff looked great. But [this was] the first time that we got to see two characters fighting with lightsabers; we had audio in there, we had all that animation in. And that was a moment of: 'Yeah, that looks fuckin' awesome.'

"We were able to see the characters in the engine and running in the game, and play around with them in a gray-box environment, but once they finally got some of the kinks worked out of that combat system, it felt *great*. For exactly what it was supposed to be, which was a real-time-input but statistically driven, dice-roll combat system. It was fluid, and it flowed, because the action would never stop. You just issued commands, and they would fight and do their thing."

Combat in *KotOR* begins, generally, as soon as an enemy spots the player's traveling party. Whether the player is using an Xbox controller or keyboard-and-mouse setup, they can pause and unpause the action with a single button press, issue strings of commands for each of up to three hero characters, and then watch as the battle plays out in a series of rounds. If the player doesn't issue specific commands, the combatants fight it out automatically using their default mode of attack. Characters remain more or less stationary, but they react to what enemy combatants are doing, lightsabers clashing and flaring the way filmgoers have seen them do on the big screen. As an added bonus, LucasArts supplied the authentic sound effects Ben Burtt had designed for the original movies decades earlier.

It wasn't perfect, but it looked and sounded like Star Wars. The publisher breathed a sigh of relief; its partnership with BioWare had begun to pay off. Still, they had a long road ahead of them.

"Part of my role on the LucasArts side was to make sure that I was getting what we needed to get out of the team at BioWare, but then also working with licensing and dealing with those approvals," Gallo says. "And if [Lucas Licensing said things] like, 'No, we can't—' Or, if they were to comment on design or things like that, [my job was] to push back on those things."

One of the arguments, which Gallo lost, was regarding the opening crawl at the start of the game. In the final release, the expository text places the story "four thousand years before the rise of the Galactic Empire." In the original version of the crawl, BioWare had set the game "a thousand generations" before the original *Star Wars*—a direct callback to Ben Kenobi's famous monologue about the Jedi. Licensing rejected it outright, arguing that "generations" was too nebulous a term. "They wanted it to be a more concrete number," he says.

"I think the only [notes we got from LucasArts] were early on," project director Casey Hudson remembered in an interview. "Certain things that happen in the story. For example, we started [on development] before *Attack of the Clones*, so some of the things about cloning they didn't want us to explore very much in this game. We had slightly smaller robes on the Sand People so you could see their legs, so we [had to make] them robed. And then [we were told] certain species can have only certain-colored eyeballs and little things like that."

Perhaps the biggest battle was over the various lightsaber colors that would be allowed in the game. "[Skywalker Ranch], George Lucas, and Lucasfilm were working on *Attack of the Clones*," Gallo says, "and there's a ton of lightsaber fights in that. All the good guys have blue and green lightsabers, the bad guys have red, there's *one* purple saber—that's it. There were all these crazy rules that they had. A lot of it was set up, we speculated, because it's easier to tell: 'Good guys are *this*, bad guys are *this*.' And we were told, 'You can't have any lightsaber colors besides red, blue, and green.'" But limiting the game to only three lightsaber colors proved a barrier to player customization, a hallmark of *KotOR*'s design.

"If you look at the toys that came out between *Episode I* and *Episode II*, there were a ton of Jedi that they started making during that time," Gallo recalls. "They did almost all of the Jedi that were on the Jedi Council in *The Phantom Menace*. And of course, the Jedi in the movie never had their lightsabers, but with the toys they kind of had to. Plo Koon, I think, had a yellow lightsaber, and Adi Gallia—one of the female Jedi, who had the braids—she had a red saber. And she was a *good Jedi*. And, obviously, when *Episode II* came out, any of those toys, if those characters got made again, they had blue and green lightsabers if they were Jedi.

"We had a design and a system in the game that was: get your lightsaber crystal, and change the color of it, and you can customize it and change the color of the blade. And I think we only had eight colors—but it was *kind of a big deal*. And we pushed back, and just said, 'A, this has been there forever. B, what are the rules for this? How can we play within this?' Ultimately, how we got it approved was, we just used the fact that: 'Hey, we're four thousand years before the films. We're in a totally different time frame. Isn't that enough to make it okay for us to use this? We can write some lore around it, and make that kind of part of this story.' But eventually we got the okay to use the different lightsaber colors, and there wasn't any problem if our character wanted to use a red saber, or a purple, or whatever." Having extra options would give players a sense of personal style, and become a significant part of the game's legacy, but there was still more at stake than an opening crawl or lightsaber crystals.

In trailers, and speaking to the press, BioWare had made it clear that the initial plan was to launch the game in late 2002, but internally that was never considered a realistic goal. "The biggest issue with *KotOR* was, we knew when we signed it that it wasn't gonna be on time. It wasn't gonna hit the original deadline," Gallo says. "And I think that there was kind of an agreement that, if there was an overrun, then we would have to talk about that—but from a financial standpoint, there wouldn't be penalties applied. It was always meant to be quality over everything else.

"There wasn't a feeling of dread about it. I think that people were excited about the game, and of course everybody was seeing builds and seeing the progress, so there wasn't any worry there. It was really how much longer it was going to take to wrap this thing up that was always the question. We were constantly fighting performance issues. Because there were the [d20] game systems running underneath everything, we were always fighting performance. So this isn't much different from any other game, but it's usually a difficult problem to solve. You're working on that until you put it out the door, and you're still working on it *after* you get it out the door. And, yeah, there were times where it's like,

'Wow, performance is terrible. How are we supposed to play this game?'

"We were trying to push these bigger vistas, and it had these characters that looked great, making sure that any NPC you went up to looked good. With the game system running underneath it, and then all of the audio—on something [as large as] *KotOR*, you don't want to ship it where it's kind of falling over itself."

Regardless of the design challenges and technical hurdles BioWare encountered, the developer had an ace up its sleeve that guaranteed the game would at least *look* fantastic: the art team.

ANALOG

WHAT MAKES A MOVIE, COMIC BOOK, or video game feel like Star Wars? This is the question every creator has to wrestle with when they're approached to work on a story set in that universe.

When George Lucas began working on the original *Star Wars* in the 1970s, his aim was to make a film that looked timeless—never mind the endless budgetary and technical limitations he had to contend with. Production designer John Barry and set decorator Roger Christian proposed the notion of a "used universe," a term that's come to be associated with Lucas and the success of the classic trilogy over the years. The idea was to avoid the polished chrome and utopian vistas of earlier science fiction movies in favor of something a bit more tangible: the grimy, kitbashed, lived-in aesthetic of the Mos Eisley cantina or the Millennium Falcon. Props and sets could be assembled from existing parts, and in turn the whole production would be less expensive.

BioWare insisted on following these same design principles during the making of *Knights of the Old Republic*. One look at the game's cover is all it takes to grok the similarities—the rusty flying-saucer pirate ship, the archetypal hero brandishing her laser sword, the R2-D2 and C-3PO analogues, the Universal-monster-movie villain.

"The reason I draw pictures, what galvanized me as a ten-year-old boy, was *Star Wars* on the big screen, May 25, 1977," says John Gallagher, who designed most of the game's characters and costumes. "It changed my life."

Gallagher worked in broadcasting, writing and producing television commercials, prior to joining BioWare. Like most of his peers, he was a neophyte in the games world. "But I've drawn my entire life," he says. "Anybody who knows me knows that, from the time I could hold a crayon, that's really what I was doing. It was kind of in my DNA." He spent a total of nine years with the company, witnessing its humblest beginnings and staying on until 2004, two years into development on *Dragon Age: Origins*.

KotOR is a particularly cherished memory for Gallagher because it gave him the chance to meet his hero: *Star Wars* production illustrator Ralph McQuarrie.

In 2001, following months of preparation, work on the game began in earnest. "Once the post-orgasm glow [of getting the Star Wars license] was diminishing,"

Gallagher says, "we had to get down to business." All of the team leaders on the project at BioWare flew down to the San Francisco Bay Area to spend a day with the Lucas camp. For the art team—Gallagher, lead animator Steve Gilmour, and art director Derek Watts—that meant a trip "across the pond" to Berkeley, where McQuarrie and his wife lived. There, the BioWare folks were treated like visiting dignitaries. They got to hold the Oscar that McQuarrie had won for Best Visual Effects with *Cocoon* in 1986. McQuarrie showed them his original work, offered advice, and shared stories about "George and the old days."

"That was life-changing," Gallagher says. "I got to sit at the feet of the master and spend a few hours with him. He was an extraordinary human being, and just a natural pleasure to spend time chatting with. And you feel like the circle's complete. If Ralph gives you a thumbs-up, then you feel like, *Okay, now I can go do this.* And he'd entertained diplomats and kings. I was just another asshole who drew pictures."

Most artists struggle with some degree of impostor syndrome—the fear that, no matter what they accomplish in their chosen creative field, sooner or later they'll be exposed as frauds. Even if your name is Ralph McQuarrie. Even if many credit you with envisioning the singular look of the entire Star Wars universe.

McQuarrie told Gallagher about a stroll he took one night in 1977. He liked to go for walks in abandoned spaces—at the docks, in industrial zones, in warehouse districts.

On this particular night, though, McQuarrie happened to be on Hollywood Boulevard.

"He was walking along, a little bit of a breeze blowing," Gallagher says. "Nobody else around. And this paper packet rolls by him—a little wrapper. He looks down and it's a Star Wars wrapper, for the collectible cards, with a blue-and-yellow Darth Vader on the front. Fifteen cents. It hits him in the shoe; he bends over and picks it up. Says, 'Huh. Guess I'm gonna do okay at this.'"

For Gallagher, working on *Knights of the Old Republic* wasn't just another job; it was a chance to contribute to the galactic sandbox his hero had helped dream up decades earlier. There was an enormous amount of pressure to get it right. Fortunately, McQuarrie had some words of wisdom for the artists at BioWare.

"He didn't really have to tell me this, but he said, 'Always push back. Be of service, but let them understand that they need you more than you need them,'" Gallagher remembers. "And he wasn't being confrontational or gnarly. It was just, 'Hey, man, you're an essential voice here, and your contribution means a phenomenal amount to the process.' That was his bit of advice for me, anyway: *Be your own boss, don't take their shit, and you'll be fine."*

McQuarrie also told them, "Enjoy the process itself."

Luckily, Gallagher wasn't left alone to create in a bubble. Every step of the process was a collaboration between BioWare's art, design, and writing teams; no single person was responsible for a given character.

"James [Ohlen] and I had a creative shorthand," Gallagher says, "and we'd finish each other's sentences when it came to design. James would usually just say, 'Well, make somethin' cool.'"

Growing up, Ohlen had served as Dungeon Master for his friends in Grande Prairie, Alberta, and the West End Games Star Wars RPG was a favorite pastime. "I took characters from the campaign I ran, their names and personalities and stuff, and those inspired some of the characters in *Knights of the Old Republic*—Carth, Bastila, Zaalbar, and Mission," he says. "That was a quick source of inspiration. I'd done that with the Baldur's Gate series, too, because it takes a long time to create characters sometimes. I would go back to characters that had been developed over years of playing in a role-playing game."

"Naming characters is always one of the hardest things to do," says project director Casey Hudson. "But [self-exiled Jedi] Jolee Bindo [got his name from] an imaginary friend that I had when I was three years old, that I invented. And I have no idea where that name came from, but it's just one of those that—you know, when you're searching for stuff, you just draw from your background."

The Twi'lek rogue Mission Vao "was originally supposed to be a young male, maybe a teenager or in his early twenties, based on some of the concepts that we had," according to art director Derek Watts. "But we decided to make her female." Even after settling on the character's gender, the team at BioWare continued to push for a design "more like a cute teen and less like the kid from *Terminator 2*," as Watts told *Electronic Gaming Monthly*. "Everyone was fine with the new look except for one of the writers, who thought she was painted up too much. We reminded him that he wrote a line for Mission that said, 'If you don't watch out, you'll have to deal with my furry friend.'"

Ideas usually began with BioWare's core leadership, including Hudson and Ohlen, but developers would often find other ways to incorporate pieces of themselves into the game. One example of this is Pazaak, an in-universe minigame based on blackjack.

"We wanted to have a card game, and I *am* a frequent visitor to Vegas," says writer Drew Karpyshyn. "So I was the one who actually designed the basics of how Pazaak would work, the rules system, and then worked with one of the programmers to implement it into the game."

But cardplaying wasn't the only hobby of Karpyshyn's that made its way into the project.

"I used to play on a billiards team," he says. "Four of the people on it were named Harrison—several brothers or various relatives. And we were gonna call ourselves the 'HK-41s': four Harrisons and one Karpyshyn. We said, 'Well, it sounds more like the AK-47 if we call ourselves the *HK-47s*.' So that was the name of my billiards team when I played in the league. And when they found out I was working on a Star Wars game, [my teammates] were like, 'Oh, you *have* to make a robot called HK-47.'"

In *KotOR*, players encounter the murderous protocol droid HK-47 in a junk shop on Tatooine. He's remembered fondly as a source of comic relief, as written by designer David Gaider, and also for his menacing, alien design.

For Gallagher, HK-47 was a far less personal affair. "It was a very short conversation," Gallagher says. "James just said, 'I need a badass C-3PO.' So all I did was essentially use a bilaterally symmetrical protocol-droid physique, with a little bit of enhancement and a snake head, which is really the inspiration for the broader, flatter face. And it was a copperhead, as I recall. So that's really the inspiration: He was a copperhead C-3PO. And, of course, his personality is what really carries the day, but his physical personality has to reflect his disposition."

The similarities to C-3PO didn't stop at the physical. In a nod to the more famous droid's origin story—that he'd been built by young Anakin Skywalker long before he became Darth Vader—HK-47 is revealed to have been owned by none other than Darth Revan himself.

Of course, the artists and designers working on the game didn't always agree with one another, and they weren't afraid to say so. One especially contentious character was Darth Malak, the Sith Lord hunting the player throughout the game. At some point, Malak suffered a lightsaber blow to the face; his most striking feature is a metal prosthesis where his lower jaw used to be.

"I gave James shit about [the Malak design]," Gallagher admits. "Because I thought it looked like Mort from *Bazooka Joe and His Gang*. I was like, 'What the hell is that? You should just have a turtleneck [covering his mouth]. He got his *mandible* cut off?' I was like, 'For fuck's sake, James. Really?'

"I was outvoted, obviously," Gallagher remembers. "And I didn't go away and sulk or anything. I said, 'I'm not gonna design Malak because I think it's a terrible idea.' I was designing other elements for the game, and there was a shit-ton of stuff to do, so I was just like: 'Derek probably has a good handle on this.' And we ended up with the Malak concept. It doesn't *bother* me.

It doesn't insult me. I just don't think it's a very well-realized design."

Malak aside, Gallagher's fingerprints are all over the art design in the game. He designed the vast majority of the characters—as well as many costumes, props, and vehicles.

"I probably did twenty iterations of each character, essentially, if you did a head count," Gallagher says. "As I recall, we were creating by chapter, so the people we meet first in a meaningful way, in terms of story, are the first ones you take a crack at. And once you break the neck on the core design, and you're honoring the Star Wars aesthetic while trying to add your own flourishes in there, then you move forward and cut your teeth on Revan and the Sith. Because it was Star Wars, and we were following the Star Wars methodology, where you offer a multitude of variants on each [character design]. And it's subtle permutations, where you go, 'Okay, that's the one.' Or, 'That head combined with those legs, and that works.' I was drawing it all up with marker at that point. I wasn't working digitally; it was too slow. I was just grinding out analog art."

According to Mike Gallo, some of BioWare's biggest contributions to Expanded Universe lore arose from a desire to make full use of the blank-slate nature of the Old Republic setting. Lucasfilm's licensing division had to sign off on any original creations anyway, so it allowed the two companies to collaborate, in a sense, as the process moved along. From this alchemy came planets like Manaan and new alien races like the Selkath, both of which have become lasting pieces of Star Wars lore: Manaan appeared in BioWare's MMORPG, *Star Wars: The Old Republic*, following the release of the 2014 *Galactic Strongholds* expansion. And, more notably, a member of the Selkath race was even featured in the 2008 animated television series *The Clone Wars*, which has been enshrined in the official Star Wars canon.

"I remember someone asking me about the Selkath at the Vancouver Fan Expo, and I was like, 'Yeah, I'm not gonna lie, they were *just another race*,'" Gallagher says. "And I don't mean that dismissively, but if you have a list of two hundred characters that you need to draw, you don't get particularly precious. You want to make sure you're not being derivative and you're not just knockin' them out for the sake of finishing your tasks, of course, but to say that one had more significance than another? That's never really the case when you're concept-designing. You just want to make sure that they're all singular and interesting and eye-catching, and that you can tell by their silhouette what they are, and all the usual rules of visual stylization."

The Rakata, a long-vanished race of colonialists who once wielded unimaginable power, are another of *KotOR*'s major additions to the Expanded Universe. Revan's story involves a search for the Rakata's crowning achievement: a colossal weapons factory called the Star Forge.

"We did want [to include a] precursor [species], the ancient race that has disappeared, the mysterious shapers of society," Karpyshyn says. "It's a very common archetype in narrative, and through our mythology and our cultural stories that we tell. And we wanted something that was a mystery the player could reveal and discover. I don't remember specifically how the Rakata came about, or how we decided the details of them. It was a two-year project, so a lot of these things evolve very slowly. A lot of times, there's not really a lightning-bolt moment. It's more a process of iterating and working with the team and getting everybody's input, and you just keep working at it till you get something that feels right."

"We always pushed for the best idea," Gallagher says. "We'd punch holes in bad ideas. We were just committed to doing the very best we could, in the time we had available, with the resources on hand."

"We're *so damn critical* of each other," says Ohlen. "Which is good—which is part of our secret sauce. The BioWare culture is one where people aren't afraid to give critical feedback at every single point in a project's development."

Glance at BioWare's output around the turn of the millennium, and it's clear that this company culture yielded results. In the span of eight years, the studio released a sequel to Shiny Entertainment's *MDK*; two very different but equally well-liked D&D titles; a masterful Star Wars role-playing game; an original action RPG called *Jade Empire*; and *Mass Effect*, the first entry in one of the most beloved science fiction series of all time.

Of all the designs in *KotOR*, probably the most important was Revan, the mysterious Sith Lord at the heart of the story. "James just said, 'Make it look cool; he [shouldn't] look like a regular Jedi,'" Gallagher says. "And I remembered the Mandalorian throw." Gallagher looked to fan-favorite bounty hunter Boba Fett, first introduced in *The Star Wars Holiday Special* and *The Empire Strikes Back*, for inspiration. "But he's saying, 'Make it *older*,' so I was like, *Okay, a freakin' tribal mask. Done.* And having some leather on him, which of course became a [motif for] a lot of the design. And we were holding true to that—only because it's an interesting texture, and it certainly gives a different look for characters that you're accustomed to seeing in only fabric and metal or molded plastic. So it was a very short conversation."

Gallagher notes that different characters call for different levels of depth: There are background characters who only need "to look kind of cool." There are NPCs who benefit from some light research into pop psychology. "And in the case of Revan, you wanted him to be unreadable and inscrutable, which serves the character."

The team also took a lot of inspiration from old Star Wars books and sketches. "If you look at the Star Wars guidebooks, or the Ralph McQuarrie treasury, which is magnificent, some of the little side doodles in the margins contain a lot of really interesting information. Because he was also drawing with the idea of making it timeless, in the sense that even though it's four thousand years before the rise of the Empire, it might as well have been *fifty* thousand. And he wanted it to feel that way—to be truly mythic, and of no particular era, like a fairy tale in space." That edict had originally come down from George Lucas in 1974, at the very beginning.

"McQuarrie remains the luminary," Gallagher says. "It's very easy to be inspired just by huffing his fumes. [You'll be looking at] throwaway sketches that never showed up in any of the movies, but you're like, *Oh, fuck.* That cues you on to other things. And we used a lot of that. I mean, I can't speak for any of the other artists, but I cued off a lot of his throwaways or his iteratives of certain ideas, and would just go: 'Huh, I like that. I oughta try that and see how that works out.' You want to maintain the Star Wars form language, because it needs to be recognizable—that combination of fallen low-tech and lo-fi, combined with impossible technology. It's important to stay at source, not out of fear but out of respect. I didn't want to insult the property by going, 'Oh, but my ideas are like *this*.' I didn't really want to graft any sort of personality [onto the visual design of the game]. I thought the place to do that was with characters. And that's a group effort.

"The personality, because it's an RPG and our engines were never bleeding-edge, was really about concentrating on the connective tissue in the narrative. Not necessarily, *Can I do the most amazing aliens?* And these races have all existed there. What you do is go back into the lore, which has run wild for years, and if you find things that are interesting, or kind of peculiar or offbeat, you just throw them in. So we were given carte blanche to play in the Star Wars sandbox, but I think we all wanted to make sure we were honoring what that franchise is about and what it meant to us. We didn't color out of the lines too much."

What made *KotOR* so integral to Star Wars, however, were the places where the team dared to draw new lines altogether. And when they did, it was always a team effort.

"When people say 'You created Darth Revan,' I say 'No, I didn't. I was the first person to visualize the character. To bring them to life.' The first time it's visualized and you nail a concept, then everybody dials into that and it becomes a true group effort. I mean, it was 25 people who were responsible for making Revan amazing. So of that 25, I'm one, and yeah, of course I feel some ownership. You just say, 'I'm creating a character to help tell a story, as part of a team, and each character has their own life in the world.' And the same with HK-47. Between those two, I probably have the most ownership. Because I think Carth is largely disposable; I think Calo Nord's just another goofball."

Carth Onasi is a decorated war hero of the Old Republic and the first major companion character you meet in the game. Picture a well-dressed, well-groomed Han Solo type sporting a goatee and an orange leather jacket. Calo Nord, ironically, is one of *KotOR*'s more distinctive characters from a visual standpoint, but he mostly exists to stand around acting like a hard-ass. He's a bounty hunter who wears a leather aviator's hat and round, Doc Ock–style goggles.

Gallagher's harder on Carth than some might be, but he's right in that most of the characters who endure from *Knights of the Old Republic* are a direct result of fan enthusiasm. Revan has his own official Lego minifigure and various collectible dolls because consumers voted them into existence.

"The idea for me is you offer these to fans," Gallagher says. "You don't create it in a vacuum; you offer it to a larger culture, and they decide which of your creations are going to be the ones that are elevated to the panthcon. Not me. I mean, I can think that HK-47's a really cool design, but if the world doesn't think that, well, it doesn't stop it from being a cool design—it just means that the world didn't embrace it for that.

"But in the case of video games, and especially RPGs, you have a unique opportunity to build a relationship with your characters, which of course are a group effort. And I'm happy to have been a part of the group that created Revan and HK, in particular. Even now, to this day, people that weren't even born when *Knights of the Old Republic* came out have had the opportunity to play it, and they'll swear by Revan. The next generation has spoken loudly, saying, 'This guy's *the shit.*'

"What a gift: to have not only created for Star Wars, but to have created something lasting inside of the Star Wars universe. It's mission accomplished. It's really extraordinary."

VO

WITH THE EXCEPTION OF GEORGE LUCAS, there's one name that's appeared in the credits of more Star Wars games than anyone else's: Darragh O'Farrell. For more than two decades, he's been the go-to voice-over (VO) director for Star Wars video game projects, in the LucasArts era and beyond.

O'Farrell was working in animation in Los Angeles, circa '94, when he got wind that LucasArts was on the hunt for a VO director. "The company could see things were going from floppy disk to CD-ROM," he says. "As a film company, they needed to embrace the talent side of things a little bit more, which is how I ended up starting there." O'Farrell's first game was *The Dig*, a 1995 point-and-click adventure adapted from a story by Steven Spielberg. It starred Robert Patrick, who'd played the villain in *Terminator 2*, and featured cutscenes by Lucasfilm's renowned visual-effects studio, Industrial Light & Magic. "We were used to doing games that had like 10,000 lines of [recorded] dialogue, when no other company was really doing that at the time," O'Farrell says.

What made the casting and sound departments at LucasArts unique, compared to other internal teams, was that they worked on *all* of the publisher's titles. With Star Wars games, in particular, music and sound design has always been one of the key pillars holding the larger experience together. *Knights of the Old Republic* would be no different.

"We did want to have the BioWare DNA of story, and companion characters that you cared about, and choices that had impact," lead designer James Ohlen recalls. "But we also knew this: We couldn't do something that was text-heavy like *Baldur's Gate* or *Neverwinter Nights*, because Star Wars is a very cinematic experience. And the fan expectations would be different than Dungeons & Dragons fans' expectations. They'd be less understanding of walls of text and lots of reading, which is why [*KotOR*] was the first game where all of the non-player characters had full voice-over."

O'Farrell remembers an early meeting with producer Mike Gallo and project director Casey Hudson, at which point the plan, he says, was still to do what BioWare had done in the past—a handful of spoken lines per interaction, with the majority of dialogue being displayed in text form. O'Farrell threw out a suggestion: "Why don't we record the whole thing?"

Gallo and Hudson exchanged glances.

"We can *do* that?" said Hudson.

O'Farrell nodded. "As long as there's room on the disc." He told them he'd work on getting the budget approved; they still had about a year before it would be time to go into the studio.

"It was one of the most ambitious projects that LucasArts or BioWare had ever attempted," Gallo says. "I don't think BioWare had fully voiced anything in the same way that we were doing with this game. Certainly not that size. It was a *huge* budget for us, internally. It was a massive undertaking."

LucasArts got its money's worth, however. Pull up the IMDb entry on *Knights of the Old Republic*, and you'll be greeted with a veritable who's who of the voice-over industry. O'Farrell sent audition packets to a number of Hollywood agencies, casting the game largely with veteran actors from film, television, and previous LucasArts titles. A full paper copy of the game's script could fill ten large binders; it called for about 300 speaking characters with roughly 15,000 lines of dialogue. Following a traditional casting process, a hundred or so actors filled those roles.

Recording took place at Screenmusic Studios, on Ventura Boulevard in Los Angeles, over the course of five grueling weeks. O'Farrell was joined by voice coordinator Jennifer Sloan, and the two of them worked numerous sixteen-hour days in order to ensure the audio was ready six months out from release.

The great challenge of recording a BioWare RPG became apparent almost immediately: The game's structure was, for the most part, nonlinear. Every character, therefore, was given their own unique version of the script, and each actor had to be recorded individually. "The first week that I was in LA, James [Ohlen] was there, and he had his laptop, and every so often we'd get to a point where we weren't *quite* sure which way the branching was going," O'Farrell says. "And he would jump on and dig into the code a little bit, and then we would have a clearer direction." In later weeks, writer Drew Karpyshyn also assisted with some of the sessions.

"That's something a lot of the actors were doing for the first time," Karpyshyn says. "So you really needed someone there to give them an overview of how the branching narrative works, and how the storylines are gonna play out, depending on player choices."

"It's probably one of the earliest games where I remember a character being both dark *and* light," says Jennifer Hale, who voiced the Jedi Bastila Shan. "You know, having the ability to go in either direction. I remember doing a bunch of recording, and then coming back in for another round of recording, and them saying: 'Okay, now basically she's changing sides.

She's completely shifting.' And I'm like, 'Oh! Okay. Let's do that.'"

The game's many quest lines and relationships could develop in different ways based on what the player chose to say, or depending on which planets they journeyed to first. But the player character's actions also affected their Force alignment; needless slaughter or malice could put a Jedi on the path to the dark side. Moral or immoral choices didn't merely change the game's ending but also altered the way companion characters, like Hale's, responded to the protagonist.

The character of Bastila speaks with a British accent —"Coruscanti," in the Star Wars universe. According to Hale, a Canadian-American actor, this is something that comes naturally. "I think in various dialects in my head, but British is definitely one of the primary ones, and that's always been a part of me. Since I was little, and just in the back of my head—I don't really know why. I just know it's there. And I went to a fine-arts high school [where] we studied dialects. I've put in my time. I work with coaches every now and then when I need a tune-up."

Hale's commitment to her craft is evident to even casual fans of games. She holds the Guinness World Record for "most prolific" female video game voice actor, and has voiced characters as diverse as *The Elder Scrolls Online*'s Lyris Titanborn, *Overwatch*'s Ashe, and *Mass*

Effect hero Commander Shepard (or "FemShep"), who had her own version of the Force-alignment continuum courtesy of that game's Paragon–Renegade morality system. Tom Bissell, writing for *The New Yorker*, once called Hale "a kind of Meryl Streep of the form."

"There's no end of positives that you can say about Jennifer," O'Farrell says. "Take somebody like Liam Neeson. Without him forcing it, you know, there's a strength that Neeson gives off without actually having to overtly put it out there—it's just the demeanor that's there. There's a *strength* behind it. And Jennifer has that, too. You just know that she's not somebody you want to fuck with, you know? She's a badass without having to be a badass. From a purely professional standpoint, she's just a great actor. She makes sessions easy because she's clued in and just gets it. So you can kind of jump in and start hammering out a lot of lines, and you're just getting quality the whole time."

Some of Hale's earliest credits were, in fact, Star Wars games: *X-Wing vs. TIE Fighter* (1996), *Force Commander* (2000), *Jedi Academy* (2003). "I did a ton of games early on because, frankly, a lot of actors didn't really want to do them because they were super demanding. And I just seemed to have a knack for it," Hale says. "In the early 2000s, it was really exciting to be involved in the creation of games, and kind of at the forefront of some of the really powerful cinematic stuff that was going on, and especially as a woman. To be given these powerful roles, and a place to lead, and to occupy characters that were leaders, was phenomenal."

The essence of the job, she says, "is really to go out and have as big a life as I can, and then to bring that experience into the booth."

Bastila, a young Jedi grappling with both the enormous depth of her powers and her connection to Revan, is the emotional anchor of the game. Beyond Revan, she's the beating heart of *Knights of the Old Republic*, and credit for much of the game's resonance is due to Hale's stellar work on the character.

One of the most contentious performances to come out of the production, oddly enough, was the beloved assassin droid HK-47, played by actor-director Kristoffer Tabori.

"Originally, [BioWare] wanted him really serious and evil and sinister," O'Farrell recalls. "Because of our schedules, I was basically working nine to one, taking an hour, working two to six, and then at six o'clock I would do a session until ten, and I would just kind of eat, you know, while we were working. And Kris was one of those evening sessions."

In the script, the character wasn't played for laughs. A droid with a lust for violence, HK introduces almost every new line of dialogue with a tag denoting the mode of speech. ("Expletive: *damnit*, master, I am an assassination droid—not a dictionary!") His voice is stilted, mechanical. He's also utterly misanthropic, often referring to human beings, including the player character, as "organic meatbags."

Tabori tried performing the part as written, but something was missing.

"After about twenty minutes we both, almost simultaneously, said, 'You know, I'm just not feeling this. This isn't quite working. I think we've got to play up the comedy angle,'" O'Farrell says. "And so we played around for five minutes with it, trying to sort of find the voice, and then decided, 'Okay, we've settled on something.' And we went back to the beginning of the script and recorded everything again, working our way through all of the HK-47 stuff."

Usually, over the course of that five-week stretch, O'Farrell would fly into the Bay Area on Friday night and spend the weekend at home before returning to LA to record again. One week, however, he dropped by the LucasArts office on a Monday morning, and Mike Gallo stopped him in the hallway.

"We need to talk about HK-47," Gallo said. "Everybody *hates* it."

O'Farrell told him, "Mike, look, we tried to do what was on the character sheet. It wasn't working. We went for the comedy route. I get that everybody might hate it right now, but you know what? We're up against the gun. Let me finish the entire project, and then if there's time at the end, we'll talk about it." Another month went by, and BioWare was forced to live with Tabori's tongue-in-cheek version of the droid for the time being.

When O'Farrell got back from Los Angeles, and all the initial sessions were over, he asked, "What are we going to do with this HK-47 thing?"

"Oh, everybody loves it now," Gallo insisted. "Everyone thinks it's funny. We can't cut funny."

KotOR features a fantastic mix of animation vets and onscreen actors, some of whom have become Star Wars mainstays, such as Tom Kane, who's voiced characters like Yoda in *The Clone Wars* and Admiral Ackbar in *The Last Jedi*. In this particular game, Kane plays Yoda doppelgänger Vandar Tokare.

"There's definitely some legendary talent," O'Farrell says, poring over the game's IMDb page. "It's funny, I just went to see [the movie] *Coco* this weekend with my wife and kids, and there was a trailer on—it was like, 'Oh, *there's Tom Kane.*'

"Tom's one of those amazing guys where—a lot of actors will pick one or two areas of the voice-over or acting world, and that's what they focus on. Some people do cartoons, and they dabble a little bit in ad work, but they don't have the voice or the pipes to do movie trailers. "Tom is amazing at ad copy. He has the pipes to do trailers. But he's also really good at *characters*. And so he's everywhere."

O'Farrell remembers a day in the recording studio when he learned just how versatile Kane's talents were. "I was in the studio with him, and there was something wrong with the console. So we were having a problem, and the engineer was trying to figure it out, and I started popping my head in. I was like, 'Hey, Tom, we need five minutes. We've got a little bit of a problem in here.' And so he kind of got shut off to me, and I couldn't hear him in the studio. And about five minutes later, all of a sudden—in the background I hear the *Star Wars* movie, but I'm not really focused on it. And a few minutes go by, and I turn to the engineer, and I go, 'Where is that *coming from*?' And he points to Tom, and Tom is sitting there. He's in the studio in front of the microphone, he has his legs crossed, and he is literally doing the movie line by line, character by character. And so all of a sudden I became aware: 'Oh my God, *it's Tom*.' And there's no music, there's no sound effects, there's nothing—but he's doing all the characters. And he got to the scene where it was Tarkin and Princess Leia. He's just amazing."

KotOR was also a launchpad for new VO talents, including actress Cat Taber. "When she did Mission Vao, that was her *first* [voice-over] job," says O'Farrell. "And now she does a ton of games, a ton of animation, and she was Padmé Amidala in *The Clone Wars*. People like Jennifer and Tom were already established, but she *started* [her VO career with *KotOR*]. I think she was in her early twenties."

KotOR even served as a vehicle for established film and TV actors to flex their VO muscles—as was the case with Raphael Sbarge, who played Carth. "The first time I worked with Raphael was on *Grim Fandango* [in 1998]," O'Farrell remembers. "He hadn't done a lot of voice-over prior to *Grim Fandango*, and in that game he was playing a union leader. And he was doing this one scene where he was addressing a crowd, and he kept going off-mic. Because as he was acting, he was imagining the crowd in front of him, and so he would turn to his left and then turn to his right, and he'd only be on-mic a third of the time. But when I told him to stand still, his performance level dropped. What we ended up doing is, we put three microphones in front of him—one to his left, one in the middle, and one to the right. And so we ended up catching everything. By the time he got to *Knights of the Old Republic*, he realized what he'd been doing wrong from a mic-technique standpoint, so he was spot-on."

Sbarge's performance as Carth Onasi exudes an effortless charisma, but is also defined by the memories of wartime that haunt the character. Carth is a complex hero, underrated by many fans. Sbarge is not a big-name actor, but his voice is recognizable in most roles, from *Mass Effect*'s Kaidan Alenko to television parts like George Lowery in *Bates Motel*, in which he reenacts an iconic scene from Alfred Hitchcock's *Psycho*.

Perhaps the most surprising actor to show up in *KotOR* was TV legend Ed Asner. Asner wasn't originally cast in the role of Vrook Lamar, but he ended up lending his voice to the grumpy old Jedi Master anyway.

"An actor called Pat Fraley, who is another big animation guy, did a lot of big stuff in the '80s," O'Farrell says. "And so I had Pat penciled to come in, and I called him and was like, 'Hey, look, can you work on a Saturday? Because we're running out of time; we're right at the end; I need you to do this.'"

"Yeah, yeah, fine, no problem," Fraley said. "I'll be there on Saturday."

O'Farrell handed him three character sheets, one of which was for Master Vrook. "And so on the character sheet," O'Farrell says, "he saw 'Ed Asner.'" The name had been put down not as a casting recommendation, but as a reference point for how the character might sound. Nobody expected Lou Grant from *The Mary Tyler Moore Show* to drop by for a video game gig, though Asner *had* once voiced Jabba in the radio dramatization of *Return of the Jedi*.

"Hey," said Fraley, "let me just call Ed."

Had he lost his mind? O'Farrell shook his head. "Pat. No, no, no, no, no, no, no, no. What are you talking about?"

"Yeah, yeah," Fraley said. "Ed lives across the street from me. If you want Ed Asner, let me have Ed Asner come over."

"No, no, no, we can't. *Stop*," O'Farrell pleaded. "We can't afford it."

Fraley was already dialing. "Don't worry about the money—don't worry about it."

O'Farrell said, "Put your phone down."

"Hey, Ed. Where are you?" Fraley asked. "Hey, look, I'm over at Screenmusic. I'm about to record a character that's modeled after you. Why don't you come down and do it?"

Ten minutes later, Ed Asner arrived at the studio.

O'Farrell said, "What am I gonna *pay* him?"

"I don't care," said Fraley. "As long as it's not more than you're paying me!"

"And so Ed comes in, and he goes behind the mic," O'Farrell says. "He's got the script. I explain to him, you know, the Jedi, and he kind of looks at me, sort of puzzled. And I'm like, 'The Alec Guinness sort of thing.' And he's like, 'Oh, *yeah, yeah, yeah.*'

"He's in there chewing gum, and I'm too scared to say anything. And Pat Fraley's sitting there, and he's like, 'Hey, Ed. Get your gum!' And so Ed Asner takes his gum out, throws it in the trash, and he just starts recording. And I think that character was maybe about two hours' worth of work; it wasn't that long. But he just comes out, and we start chatting, and I'm scared. I'm putting the paperwork in front of him, and I'm just terrified. And he's just chatting away; he doesn't even look down at the paperwork. He just continues to chat, and he signs his name on the dotted line.

"And that was it. Off he goes. Then Pat and I stayed on for another couple of hours, just finishing up."

Asner was a huge get for LucasArts, but Fraley had given up a juicy role to make it happen. Fraley ended up voicing Dak Vesser, a Sith trainee on the planet Korriban, along with the Tarisian cardplayer Gelrood. Blink and you'll miss him.

"The Ed Asner role was the bigger role that he had to do," O'Farrell says, "but he wanted to give it to Ed."

SLEHEYRON

WHEN LUCASARTS FIRST ANNOUNCED *Knights of the Old Republic* in a July 2000 press release, the publisher described the project as "the first Star Wars role-playing game (RPG) for PC and next-generation video game systems." This was just four months after Microsoft had unveiled its plans to enter the console arena with the first Xbox. The game's release window was slated for 2002. But between Interplay going bankrupt during development on *Neverwinter Nights* and *KotOR's* massive scope, the Xbox version of BioWare's big Star Wars game was ultimately delayed to July 2003; the PC edition would land in November. That was assuming, of course, everything went as planned.

There's a sequence in *Revenge of the Sith* where Anakin Skywalker and Obi-Wan Kenobi have just slain the Sith Lord Count Dooku and rescued Chancellor Palpatine (yet another Sith, unbeknownst to them). The galaxy-spanning conflict known as the Clone Wars is coming to an end, and all that's left is to bring the Jedi-hunting cyborg General Grievous to justice. The warship they're on, the Invisible Hand, is in freefall above the planet Coruscant. Its droid crew have either abandoned ship or been destroyed. A barrage of turbolaser fire has breached the ship's hull, and gravity's beginning to pull the Separatist flagship apart.

"Can you fly a cruiser like this?" Kenobi asks.

Anakin says, "You mean, 'Do I know how to land what's left of this thing?'"

Reentry rattles the vessel as they burn their way through the atmosphere, leaving a trail of scattered fragments in their wake. Like the Titanic, the ship splits crosswise, and its aft section breaks loose completely.

"Not to worry," Kenobi says. "We are still flying *half* a ship."

Game development's a lot like that scene, unfortunately, and titles are often shipped half broken or incomplete due to the pressures and constraints placed on studios. *Knights of the Old Republic* had the benefit of a generous production timeline, but BioWare still had to jettison some of its content before launch.

"We did cut an entire planet that we'd actually developed and built part of," says lead designer James Ohlen. "That was a difficult decision because the art for it was being built by one of my best friends, Dean Andersen. Having to cut his world was particularly painful. But it was simply a time thing. It was a gladiatorial world where the player was going through sort of a *Planet Hulk*–style plot. The player would get stuck fighting their way up through the ranks until they won the tournament and escaped off-world. But that was too much to do in the time we had, so it got cut."

Over the years, data miners have tried to glean as much info as possible about the lost planet, which was called Sleheyron. The modding community has also made several efforts to restore some of it, but there's really not much left to recover; it's mostly fan-fiction fodder at this point. However, Sleheyron is still mentioned briefly in the game.

According to a November 2001 forum post by writer David Gaider, Sleheyron's quest lines were mostly finished when the decision to cut the planet was made. Like Tatooine, Taris, or Nar Shaddaa, Sleheyron was under the influence of the slug-like gangsters known as the Hutts. ("One of them was named Suuda the Hutt," Gaider wrote. "He was very catty.") Fans can still see an approximation of this scenario in Marvel's *Star Wars* #10 (2015), by Jason Aaron. In that comic, Luke Skywalker is placed in a gladiatorial event on Nar Shaddaa to die for the amusement of a Hutt who's obsessed with Jedi artifacts. Mention of Sleheyron itself can also be found in Fantasy Flight Games's *Star Wars: The Force Awakens* Beginner Game, a stand-alone tabletop RPG released in 2016. Early screenshots published in 2002 by IGN offer a rudimentary glimpse of the lost world, which most closely resembles *The Last Jedi*'s casino planet, Cantonica.

"Those decisions are not too difficult," former LucasArts producer Mike Gallo explains. "It's like, 'Hey, here's what we're gonna do. This planet, this environment—we can't afford to build it. But there's some quests here that we're gonna move to *this* planet.'"

"Generally, that kind of shit is gonna get cut in design before we ever start digging in," says concept-art lead John Gallagher. "That happened on every game; there were plenty of areas that got smoked out in *Baldur's Gate*. And [usually] that happens in design, where it's cheapest to have it get killed. By the time it gets to [the artists], it's pretty much decided that it's locked. So there's an advantage to that process. Some studios are a little more organic and fluid, and you can get burned pretty good, but we were pretty structured even back then. Ray [Muzyka]'s a big believer in heavy, heavy front-load on design. You make all your decisions there. Once you have your design doc locked, then it's a death march, and you get the damn game done."

KotOR's development closely followed Muzyka's plan-then-create strategy. "I don't think there were any real tough decisions we had to make in terms of what was gonna be part of the game and what wasn't," Gallagher said. "We were all pretty dialed in on what we wanted, and we had the density of a dying star in there. The vast majority did end up in the game, because it's quite a dense experience in terms of visual beats. We pushed the engine to the edge of its efficiency. I think we were at a hundred and five percent overclocked, probably pushing more than it should have rightly handled, but we lucked out and got a lot of stuff working."

With deadlines looming, though, other pressures began to mount.

"I kind of moved up to Edmonton in February of 2003," Gallo recalls. "Basically, I lived up in Edmonton from February until about mid-June. I came back for a couple weeks, but spent about four months up there. Essentially, it was just making sure that we were getting stuff delivered if there was anything that the team needed. Getting into arguments, getting into fights about bugs, and all this other stuff. And we were all— you're so close to it, you're terrified. *We were terrified!* Because we knew that so much was riding on it.

"The day we first submitted to Microsoft, I also found a major crash bug in the opening tutorial, and we had to pull the submission. So, I mean, there's always those moments of terror, right?"

"It was a nightmare," BioWare cofounder Ray Muzyka told an interviewer. "I think we found 39,000 bugs. That's the most bugs we've ever had in a game."

In April or May of 2003, as the team neared the home stretch, Gallo sat down with Casey Hudson and some of the other project leads to discuss a final timetable for testing the Xbox version of the game and readying it for launch. BioWare was prepping a build to deliver to Microsoft's Xbox lab for intensive focus testing, LucasArts was expecting a report on the team's progress, and July 2003 was right around the corner. During the meeting, Gallo presented Hudson with a schedule intended to ensure the game shipped when LucasArts needed it to, while also leaving sufficient time to test the final product. To BioWare, the timeline sounded impossible. Hudson was not pleased.

"So we had a little bit of intense negotiations around that the next day," Gallo says. "I wasn't confident that we were gonna be able to fix all the bugs that we had in the time remaining, and the team really had to kind of go into super-crunch mode to make it happen."

Despite that argument, Gallo developed a deep admiration for Hudson, noting that the young project director went above and beyond the responsibilities of his role as a creative lead. "He is one of *the* most talented people that I think I've ever worked with in this industry," Gallo says. "Casey was *the guy*. He was the glue that held it together. He knew the ins and outs of the characters, the story, the music, the art direction, the art, the tech. He was truly the creative visionary of that project, along with James [Ohlen].

"James was primarily responsible for story and story structure. He's one of those guys who's very much on top of things. I mean, he is an *expert* in his field. It was always a positive experience talking to him. He's a pretty quiet guy, in a lot of ways, but he was always smiling and trying to think of cool things to do, and how they were gonna structure it and build it."

Gallo was also awed by Karpyshyn's output as a writer. "When I spent all that time up there, we used to laugh about Drew, because he would go off and write a four-hundred-page book over a weekend. 'Oh, I've got a book I've got to write.'

"For me, those are the things that are *amazing*. To see a team working like that—I will never forget it. We worked overtime, but BioWare had a pretty strict schedule toward the end to protect the team [from burnout] as much as possible."

Still, the final week was a blur of nonstop playtesting and bug-fixing. "Everyone on that team was in the office playing the game until the sun came up," Gallo remembers. "I was walking around at like 4:30 one morning, and there was an artist who had been finished with his work for *weeks*. And he was just playing through it to find bugs. I've certainly worked on teams that were great, before and since that, but it was something special."

It was an enormous relief when the team officially turned the game in to Microsoft, but there was still a lot of work to be done to deliver the PC version.

"The PC edition was a crazy finish," says Gallo. "Back in the day, we actually used to have to put people on an airplane and then fly them out. We had to have one of our localization guys take the German masters and fly the replicator into Germany because there was no way to get the discs there in time, and it was too big to send over the internet. Now you can transfer fifty gigs in thirty minutes, and I'm sure that most developers have fantastic upload and download speeds. But back then, we literally were like: 'Okay, if we start to transfer this, it's gonna take like forty-eight hours. If we can put you on a plane and have you there in twelve, we're puttin' you on a plane.'"

Crunch only worsened as the PC release got closer. "Towards the end of the PC version, we were working several all-nighters," Gallo says. "I was in a meeting with all of our ops people at LucasArts, and at one point one of the guys whispered to me: '*Mike.* You were talking, but you would fade out for five or ten seconds and then pick up again.' I'm like, 'Dude, I haven't slept in forty-eight hours.' He's like, 'What are you *doing*?' I said, 'Well, you know, that's what we do.'"

It's easy to imagine how, under such stressful conditions, creative differences and interpersonal tensions might have come to a head. Needless to say, not everyone at BioWare saw eye-to-eye all the time. "But regardless of that," says John Gallagher, "what we ended up with in that dialectic was some phenomenal work."

This creativity was enabled, in part, by the team's after-work hangouts. Throughout production, the team often left work together after dark, exhausted, hungry, and looking to blow off steam.

"The area that BioWare was in was Whyte Avenue, and they were in the upper floors of a building that was right in the middle of all this, you know, *night life*," Gallo says. "At the end of that street was the Alberta hospital, and then the University of Alberta, so there were tons of clubs and bars and places to eat. Usually, it was myself and the QA team that was down there with me from Lucas, but a few times we went out with some of the guys from the [*KotOR*] team and hung out, and just had food or drinks. And we pretty much did that almost every night after work."

"We got paid once a month, and the following Saturday after payday—because we got paid on Friday, usually towards the end of the month—we would all go out drinking and dancing," Gallagher says. Dozens of artists, designers, producers, programmers, and testers would trudge through the snow to the Whyte Avenue pubs, get a buzz going, then wind up at the nightclubs. Dizzy and drowning in bass, their vision blurred, they'd form a circle on the dance floor. And, one by one, they'd take turns busting out their best moves.

"The fuckin' *funniest shit*. Just dynamite," says Gallagher. "And the bonding that happened during these bizarre exercises lasts a lifetime. People never forget that. You know, you're in the war. And it's not until much later—I'm a regular featured guest at comic-book cons now, and comic culture obviously flows back and forth fluidly with video games. And it's not until people tell me that *Knights of the Old Republic* changed their life, that it was the game that inspired them to go into the games industry, or to pick up a pencil and start drawing...

"You never find that out, of course, when you're cloistered away in your bunker. Or when you're dancing."

THE HEART OF
THE FORCE

DEEP IN THE BELLY of a mammoth warship called the Leviathan, in a narrow red-lit corridor, a Sith Lord approaches. Jeremy Soule's menacing score thunders along. The camera follows Darth Malak and swivels around behind him to reveal the player's Jedi hero and their closest allies, Bastila Shan and Carth Onasi. This is the end of *KotOR*'s second act: This is where you learn the truth.

"Down you go!" Carth hollers, opening fire on Malak with a blaster.

Malak's scarlet blade flares to life in the dimness. Using the lightsaber, he deflects the bolts with ease, then hits Carth with a Force shove, knocking him to the floor. The Dark Lord cackles.

"I had to see for myself if it was true," Malak tells you. "Even now, I can hardly believe my eyes. Tell me, why did the Jedi spare you? Is it vengeance you seek at this reunion?"

He says, "Surely some of what you once were must have surfaced by now."

This is the big *Prestige* moment: the climactic montage that shows the audience all the pieces one last time, and lets them consider the inevitability of the twist. *So many clues; it should've been obvious.* But for many players, this kind of revelation was utterly shocking to experience in a video game.

"Jedi do not believe in killing their prisoners," Bastila explains in one memory fragment. "No one deserves execution, no matter what their crimes."

In another, Carth says, "They say the Force can do terrible things to a mind. It can wipe away your memories and destroy your very identity."

Ed Asner's character, in retrospect, comes closest to spilling: "The lure of the dark side is difficult to resist. I fear this quest to find the Star Forge could lead you down an all-too-familiar path."

"What greater weapon is there," Bastila reflects in yet another flashback, "than to turn an enemy to your cause? To use their own knowledge against them?"

The camera circles Darth Revan, now—one of the most fearsome Sith the galaxy ever faced. Revan stands surveying Rakata Prime, an ancient and forgotten world rich with the power of the dark side. As they slowly remove their mask, the sun setting behind them, the camera closes in on the face beneath: the one you chose for yourself at the start of the game. Revan's eyes, however, are a fiery yellow.

"You cannot hide from what you once were, Revan," Malak says.

Compare this carefully crafted scene to the horror and neo-noir films of the period, and it's no surprise to learn that BioWare was greatly inspired by movies outside of Star Wars.

"Darth Revan is essentially the player," says James Ohlen. "He's not meant to be a character so much as a vessel for the player to create his own character, his own version, his hero. He's a plot twist.

"We looked at a lot of the movies that had come out recently with great twists. M. Night Shyamalan's *The Sixth Sense* and *Fight Club* were two movies that we watched and saw how they developed a twist and made the grand reveal, and one of the lessons we learned— which allowed *us* to make a good twist—was that ten percent of the audience needs to figure out your twist before it happens. Otherwise, you're not giving enough clues, and the twist will come across as forced or false. You have to actually give enough clues that, when you finally make the reveal, everyone is like, 'Oh, that totally makes sense. It all comes together. I should've seen that!' And when you do give that number of clues, a large number of the audience *will* figure it out. I think where people go wrong is when they're like, *Yeah, but if they* figured it out, they'll be like, 'Oh, I saw that twist coming. That was dumb.' That's *totally okay*. Because there's a lot of people who watched *The Sixth Sense* and could see the twist coming. They were looking for the clues, and they saw them.

"And because it was Star Wars, because *Empire Strikes Back* was such a huge influence, it just felt like we needed to have that 'twist moment' in *Knights of the Old Republic*. The Darth Vader reveal is such a big part of popular culture—'*I am your father*.' That's part of what makes Star Wars, *Star Wars*. So we felt that if we did a role-playing game where there wasn't a huge reveal that changed everything the player knew, it just wouldn't feel true to Star Wars."

"I took a lot of inspiration from *The Sixth Sense*," Drew Karpyshyn recalls. "The way they revealed their twist was something we really wanted to build on. We wanted to make sure that everything was *there*, and that it was something where we could show people the groundwork we had done the way *The Sixth Sense* did. They show you all the little bits and pieces to help you put it all together. And that's something we wanted to make sure we did as well."

"It had to have your character's face," says Mike Gallo. "The character that you had built and customized *had* to be the character that was revealed in that cutscene. So we had this huge technical hurdle to sort out. And the solution that we had for that was, part of the cutscene was done pre-rendered and part of it was done in real time to make sure that it paid off.

"There may have been some people that kind of saw it coming, but it was one those things where you had built and lived with that character, and made choices to be light or dark, and then you had this twist—and you still had these big decisions that you could make, even after that, that shaped where you were going. And that's why that character was your own. Because if you played through it and it wasn't spoiled for you, you had that moment like, 'Holy shit!'"

Star Wars: Knights of the Old Republic hit store shelves on July 15, 2003, becoming, up to that point, the fastest-selling original Xbox title. The game received universal acclaim, with most reviewers citing the story, including the twist, as a key selling point.

Today, Kieron Gillen writes comics like Marvel's flagship *Star Wars* series. But in 2003, when *KotOR* hit, he was penning reviews for Eurogamer. "I hate Star Wars," Gillen wrote at the time.

Still, that didn't stop him from falling in love with *KotOR*. "I care about the Sith and the Jedi. I care about the fate of Tatooine. I care about the plight of the Sand People. I care about Wookiees who've submitted to their rage. I care about the Mandalorians," he said. "In short, *Knights of the Old Republic* takes something that's been merchandised, franchised, and branded to death over the last twenty-five years and makes it magical again."

In late 2017, I reached out to Gillen on Twitter to see how he felt about the review in hindsight. "It's a strange journey," he says. "That review was very much a piece of structuralist writing. I was writing for the hardcore gamers, and there had been a lot of shit Star Wars games in the previous few years, plus the [response to the prequels]. So doing an 'I hate Star Wars' as a tactical gambit, as a way to explain how good *KotOR* is, was very much me being me." Tactic or not, Gillen wasn't alone in suggesting that *KotOR* was the most enjoyable Star Wars product in years.

"With my brand of Star Wars fan, who I am as a fan, I've always just been pleasantly surprised and maybe even a little shocked when things would be coming together," says Darth Maul voice actor Sam Witwer. "I remember when *X-Wing* came out, and I just couldn't wrap my brain around why anyone wanted to make a flight simulator set in the Star Wars universe. It just didn't make any sense; Star Wars was *done*. When it came to *Knights of the Old Republic*, the prequels were coming out, so at that point it was a little bit more expected that you would see Star Wars products.

"But a *role-playing game*—that was a concept that I feel like was targeted directly at me, because I've been a huge fan of all Star Wars role-playing games since the original West End Games. That's how I kind of became a rabid fan: reading the West End Games books and learning about the universe through all that. And simply the scope of it. You're expecting kind of a *Baldur's Gate*–sized thing, and we *got that*. BioWare did a good job of creating the illusion that you had the run of the galaxy a little bit.

"And I did not see the twist coming. I just remember being super excited by the idea that this was a guy who related to both the dark side and the light, in his own way. In fact, Revan was supposed to appear in one of the *Clone Wars* episodes that we worked on." That scene, in which Witwer played a character called the Son, was cut from the final episode (season three's "Ghosts of Mortis"). But rough, unfinished footage of Revan's appearance and dialogue can still be found online.

Walt Williams, a video game writer best known for his work on *Spec Ops: The Line* (2012) and *Star Wars Battlefront II* (2017), drew on his experience playing *KotOR* when it came time to craft a twist ending of his own.

"The choice at the end of *KotOR* very much inspired that entire climax in *Spec Ops*," Williams says. "Because, for me, that's the thing that video game morality misses— is the ability to look at yourself honestly and decide if you want to make a change for the better or worse. Where, in other video games, everything's a blanket score of, *Well, we can't go back and change the past; this is just what you are.* It's very much an engineer's guide to morality. Very straightforward, slightly sociopathic. But for those of us more inclined towards the literary arts, that moment of reconciliation and that moment of choice is what's so important. And with *KotOR*, that really being the choice of: *Do I want to be better? Or do I want to—I almost conquered the world once. Fuck, I bet I can probably do it. Who gets a second shot at this? Not many. Let's wrap this up!* That's an amazing choice. To this day, it's still right on top of my favorite choices in a game, and one of my absolute favorite twists."

On May 4, 2004, LucasArts announced a sequel. Obsidian Entertainment—a new company in Irvine, California, founded by former employees of *Icewind Dale* developer Black Isle Studios—would take the reins from BioWare.

According to James Ohlen, BioWare cofounders Ray Muzyka and Greg Zeschuk had made the decision to pass on *Knights of the Old Republic II: The Sith Lords*. "In order for a company to be successful and control its own destiny, you need to own your own IP," Ohlen told Eurogamer, "and we didn't own Dungeons & Dragons or Star Wars. *Mass Effect* was something we decided we had to do instead of another Star Wars game."

"BioWare didn't want to do it on the timeframe that we wanted it," says Mike Gallo. "They knew that they would've been under the gun. I mean, they'd just made a game of the year, and they didn't want to sign up to make something that was less than that." The notion of a one-year development cycle was antithetical to *KotOR*'s quality-first directive. "That being said, they were *great* partners. Obsidian had a huge relationship with BioWare before they broke off, because they were all Interplay and Black Isle guys. So there was a lot of collaboration between BioWare and Obsidian in the early days of that game."

"We also had plans for a *Knights of the Old Republic II* before we gave it over to Obsidian, and I remember one of the storylines," Ohlen says. "In trying to think of a twist that would be powerful, because it was gonna be hard to top the Darth Revan twist, one of the ideas was: 'What if we made the villain the most unlikely person to be the villain?' What we wanted to do was to take the Yoda race, which we had one of in *Knights of the Old Republic*, and have the main character in *Knights of the Old Republic II* be trained by a member of that race. And that would be his mentor and quest-giver and essentially the most trusted person in the galaxy. Then, halfway through the game, it would've been revealed that the Yoda figure was actually not a member of the light side, and he'd been training the player for evil purposes. Basically, the twist was, 'Holy crap—Yoda's *evil*?' But Obsidian went with their own story."

"In the time from when *Knights of the Old Republic II* shipped until I left," Gallo says, "there were at least two different pitches for *KotOR III*. And one of them was an internal [LucasArts] pitch, and one of them was an Obsidian pitch. And at that point leadership had turned over at Lucas, and that was kind of one of the moments of change where [LucasArts was saying], 'Hey, look, we're gonna do games for mass market.' Because *Knights of the Old Republic* was not seen as a mass-market game, and it really wasn't. It had its fans, and it sold a tremendous amount of units for the time, but it was not a mass-market game. It wasn't *Battlefront*.

"And that's what [the 2004] *Battlefront* became. *Battlefront* was kind of the first 'next big thing' that LucasArts wanted to do. And the first one was huge, and the second one was *way* bigger than the first one. So I think that was the shift. If anything, maybe *Knights* kind of opened a little bit of the door. I go back to that initial goal for *Knights*: Make it the best Star Wars game we can. We want it to be a *good game*, and a good Star Wars game. Had that game not been very good, or had it not been reviewed as well as it was, it could have been a very different story for LucasArts."

MASS SHADOW

The night the team submitted *Knights of the Old Republic* to Microsoft for certification, Mike Gallo didn't sleep a wink. He left Edmonton and flew home to California the very next morning, spent several days sleepwalking around the office at LucasArts, and then he was off for another adventure: San Diego Comic-Con.

The third week of July 2003, just as players were getting their hands on *KotOR* for the first time, Gallo and fellow producer Haden Blackman were charged with manning the LucasArts booth at Comic-Con. Stormtroopers and superheroes alike swarmed the convention center, eager to catch a glimpse of the entertainment industry's biggest coming attractions. Original Boba Fett actor Jeremy Bulloch was on-site signing autographs. The publisher had set up playable demos of *Star Wars Galaxies*, *Racer Revenge*, *Rogue Squadron III: Rebel Strike*, *Jedi Knight: Jedi Academy*, and of course *Knights of the Old Republic*. DK Publishing, Paizo, and StarWars.com were selling books, magazines, and Hyperspace subscriptions to fans who were already thirsty for the slightest drop of info about *Star Wars: Episode III*. Someone had hung a large *Attack of the Clones* banner that read, *Size Matters Not—Except on an IMAX Screen!*

Still in the throes of burnout from bringing the game to market, Gallo had a tough time matching fan enthusiasm. "It was really difficult. Very strange," Gallo recalls. "I had done a million trade shows and E3s and comic cons, and this one was one of the most difficult ones I ever had to work because I had just finished working on this thing. We'd just shipped it, it had gone gold—and then I had to help people *play* it? I was like, 'I don't wanna watch *anybody* play this game.'"

The LucasArts PR team had arranged for Gallo and Blackman to do a panel, as well, speaking about upcoming Star Wars games to an audience of hundreds.

"And it didn't hit me until we were sitting up on that stage," Gallo says, "and there was someone sitting right in the front row who had a T-shirt on that said: *I heart Carth*. Which was Carth Onasi from the game. That was the moment where I was like, *Holy shit. This means a lot to people. They care about this stuff.* And at the next Comic-Con, there were cosplayers dressed up as Malak and Bastila—and you still see that *today*. I was such a small part of that thing, and it's become such a huge part of my life."

"That Revan persists, and HK-47 persists, is remarkable," says John Gallagher. "We didn't think we'd ever create anything that would not only persist but flourish. And I think in the case of Revan, especially, he's kind of timeless. I get people coming to my booth, and I pose for pictures with Revan. A friend sent me pictures of custom sculpts they've done of HK-47. Another friend of mine, Paul Harding, did a Darth Revan statue for Gentle Giant Studios, and did a fantastic job. So these are all honors and privileges—to see your work, and work that you've been a part of, kept alive by the fandom is really unbelievable."

Molly Chu, a cosplayer from San Francisco, became aware of *KotOR* in 2016, shortly after *The Force Awakens* made her a Star Wars fan. "A lot of fans were pointing out how the characters of Bastila and Revan were kind of similar to Rey and Kylo," she remembers, "so I started playing the game, and I thought Bastila's story was really interesting—that she fell to the dark side and was brought back by someone who was also once on the dark side." Chu spent half a year collecting references of the in-game model, searching for the right fabric, and carefully sewing together layers of vinyl to reproduce the intricate designs. "Her outfit is very different from a typical Jedi, and I saw a lot of Asian influence in its design, so that was appealing to me," Chu says. She's been surprised by the number of people who have approached her at conventions to express their affection for the character.

One such fan had a son named Revan.

The thematic and visual similarities between Rey and Bastila, or between Kylo Ren and Revan, have been a fascination among Star Wars fandom since even before *The Force Awakens* hit theaters in December of 2015. Flip through the recent art books that chart the making of the Star Wars sequel trilogy, and you'll note that most of the "Jedi Killer" villain concepts bear little resemblance to the Kylo that ultimately wound up on the big screen. Kylo's mask does, however, look decidedly Revan-esque.

"I like to *think* it was influenced by it," says Drew Karpyshyn. "I like to feel that we've become part of Star Wars and had some impact on the overall franchise in that way. I don't know if that's true; this is just what I like to believe. But the interesting thing about working on something like Star Wars is that everything's influenced by everything else, and it traces back and back and *back*. So obviously Revan has shades of Darth Vader, and Malak does, too. Things trace back to the films—and even the Star Wars films had their own set of inspirations.

"Creatively, you have to understand that people are going to take bits and pieces and use them, especially in a shared universe like Star Wars. And, personally, I'm flattered when I see things like that. Whether it was conscious, subconscious, or even a coincidence—I don't know. But I like to believe it was a little tip of the cap in our direction."

"That's a curious thing," says Gallagher, "because everybody co-opts, hijacks, rips off, pirates, homages. If you think that there's a pure concept designer in the world—we're all fuckin' *mongrels*, and to think otherwise is folly. Because they have access to all canon, that's their right and privilege. You're allowed to plunder as you see fit, just like we did."

"With the Kylo Ren mask, it's hard to say," says James Ohlen. "*Was it* inspired by Revan? It could have been. It definitely wasn't supposed to have anything to do with Revan, I'm sure. Personally, I was more excited by the Hammerhead, though I did miss it the first time I watched the movie." During the large space battle at the climax of *Rogue One*, the fish-faced Admiral Raddus orders a rebel corvette to ram an Imperial star destroyer. The design of that corvette is lifted directly from the Republic capital ships created for *Knights of the Old Republic.* The Endar Spire, where the player character awakens at the very start of the game, is a Hammerhead-class vessel.

"The director of *Rebels*, Dave Filoni, has gone on record—and I've even talked to him about this—saying how he's enjoyed taking some of the vehicles and items from the Old Republic era and putting them into his series," Ohlen adds. "And *Rogue One* took the Hammerhead from that show and put it into the movie, so I think that was more of a direct influence."

The characters, creatures, and worlds of *Knights of the Old Republic* seem to live on in every corner of the ever-expanding Star Wars universe. Karpyshyn authored a 2011 novel called *Revan*, which bridged the plot of *KotOR II* with that of *The Old Republic*, BioWare's $200 million MMO. Aside from holding the distinction of being one of the most expensive games ever made, *The Old Republic* also set the Guinness World Record for being the largest entertainment voice-over project of all time, with more than 200,000 lines of recorded dialogue in the base game alone. In 2014, the massively multiplayer pseudo-sequel received an expansion called *Shadow of Revan*, an attempt to bring further closure to the prodigal knight's story. *Galaxy of Heroes*, the mobile RPG from EA's Capital Games, has introduced more than a dozen playable characters based on *Knights of the Old Republic* and its follow-ups.

And there are a lot more pieces of *KotOR* in the new, canonical era of Star Wars media than the Hammerhead corvette. Peruse a guidebook or StarWars.com's Databank, and you'll find no end of *KotOR* Easter eggs in *Rogue One* alone. (The first name of General Dustil Forell, and the last name of Cassian Andor, are probably the deepest of cuts.) Malachor, Manaan, Taris, Rakata Prime—all of these worlds are now part of the official Star Wars lore. Read Kieron Gillen's *Darth Vader* comic book run, or watch a few seasons of *The Clone Wars*, and see if you can spot the numerous lightsaber colors. So much for the doctrine of blue, green, red, and violet. Pay attention to the more sinister droids, especially in Gillen's work; HK-47's spirit certainly lives on. Listen carefully during the Han Solo mission of 2017's *Battlefront II* for a brief mention of "the Czerka job"—a direct nod to the sleazy Czerka Corporation found throughout *KotOR*.

Many of those who fell in love with the game in 2003 are now a part of Lucasfilm, or Electronic Arts, or Marvel, and their passion for the Old Republic is no secret.

"One of the main reasons we wanted to have a world-class external RPG team build this game was to create truly believable characters," says Simon Jeffery. "Ones that would extend beyond just being someone in a video game. We all talk about the *specialness* of this game, and that is real. *KotOR* was one of those once-in-a-decade experiences."

"It was a great time," Gallagher says. "Essential. It was certainly critical in my formative years as a creator. Because once you can handle Star Wars, dude, you can handle fuckin' *anything*." However, it was never a given that the project would be a success.

"We have a culture of humility at BioWare," Ohlen told me prior to leaving the company, "which means that every single game we release, I think we underestimate how successful it will be. We're *very* hard on each other. So when *Knights of the Old Republic* was coming out, it was kind of like: 'I hope this isn't a disaster, and it doesn't *end* BioWare.' Because it's very hard, also, when you're part of the development team and you're so close to the product, and you've played it so many times. I played versions of *Knights of the Old Republic* all the way through—I don't know *how* many times. Like a hundred-plus times. And it all ran together. I can't play the game at all, now, because it would just be *painful*. I played it when it was a broken pile of crap. I played it when you were running around and the levels were all scanned-in graph-paper drawings of the maps, talking to placeholder guys with placeholder text. It's really hard to have any understanding of whether it's going to be successful or not. But that continues to this day. Even our latest game of the year, *Dragon Age: Inquisition*—I don't think anyone on the team was ready for that level of success. It was a surprise."

"One of the great things about a game like *KotOR* is the depth, and it gives a lot of different players different things that they can identify with or pick as their favorites," says Karpyshyn. "But the appeal of Revan, of course, is that it's such a personal character for the player. When you discover that you *are* Revan, it really makes that character have a deeper connection to you—and the fact that you can then sort of take Revan and push him or her in the direction you want after that discovery really allows you to be in control of that character. It makes it feel like *your character*, which is, I think, why people love Revan so much."

"I love that it's a very authentic Star Wars story," says Haden Blackman. "The struggle between good and evil, the varied cast of characters, and the sense of humor are all true to the best Star Wars films. And for its time, the game felt epic—like several films in one."

BioWare also understood that that epic feeling came, in large part, from the sense of agency the game afforded players. "One of my favorite memories is actually a moment with Mission," says Casey Hudson, "where I'm heading back to the hangar after a quest, and just as the hangar door opens, Mission stops me and says: 'Hey, wait. If we're gonna get on the ship, I have a thing that I want to do.' And she mentions something that *she* wants to do. And I'm thinking, 'I can go anywhere in the Star Wars universe—where *do* I want to go?' To me, that's the magic of that game, and something that I would love to see in the Star Wars universe again."

"We were literally assembling the plane as we were flying it," Gallagher says. "And we did our best to make it organized and structured, but there was still a lot of flying by the seat of our fuckin' pants and just trusting instinct and gut reaction and sheer temerity. Drive and perseverance. Half the time, that was our gasoline. And eighteen-hour days of monotonous regularity, too. I wouldn't fuckin' do it *now*, I tell you what. I'm an old spoiled son of a bitch now, but back then we just knew that if you elbow-greased it enough, and paid close enough attention to it, and stress-tested it, and looked for fractures and breaks in it, you could solve these problems. It was like our own little space program."

"You never know how it's gonna hit," Gallo says. "The fact that we're talking about this thing fourteen years later? It's a big deal to me. There's a part of me that feels supremely blessed to have ever been a part of that, and then another part that's like, 'I was never able to deliver anything *better than that, damnit.*' With how long I'd been working in that industry, there was part of me that's like, 'I don't want to talk about *KotOR* anymore. Let's go make another game we're gonna want to talk about instead.' But in that time, I've kind of realized, hey, you know what? I can still be happy with *KotOR* and my little piece of involvement that I had in it."

Following the *Revenge of the Sith* game in 2005, Gallo left LucasArts; but he returned briefly to the galaxy far, far away years later as a project director on Kabam's short-lived mobile game *Star Wars: Uprising*. After spearheading the blockbuster Star Wars title *The Force Unleashed* and its sequel, Haden Blackman went on to found his own development studio, Hangar 13, and served as the director of *Mafia III*. Former LucasArts president Simon Jeffery owns an independent game consultancy in San Francisco. James Ohlen, who left BioWare in July of 2018, has begun publishing his own D&D sourcebooks under the banner of Arcanum Worlds. For more than a decade, John Gallagher has worked as a freelance illustrator in the film-and-television industry; Warner Bros. regularly hires him on projects like *The Flash* and *Supergirl*. Writer Drew Karpyshyn has also gone freelance off and on in recent years, penning a series of original fantasy novels called the Chaos Born trilogy and contributing occasionally to the *Old Republic* MMO. Darragh O'Farrell is still the go-to voice director for big-budget Star Wars games, from *The Old Republic*'s expansions to 2017's *Battlefront II* campaign. After a two-year stint at Microsoft, Casey Hudson returned to BioWare in 2017 to head the studio as general manager, overseeing development of a new IP called *Anthem* as well as the next chapters in the *Dragon Age* and *Mass Effect* series.

Some of these men haven't seen each other for more than a decade, but they all speak of their time on *Knights of the Old Republic* with the same immeasurable fondness. It's not lost on them that, collectively, they changed the face of Star Wars—*and* role-playing games—forever.

Mike Gallo's voice cracks when he tells me, "It was awesome."

ACKNOWLEDGMENTS

A heartfelt thanks to LucasArts alums Mike Gallo, Haden Blackman, Simon Jeffery, and Darragh O'Farrell; former BioWare devs James Ohlen, John Gallagher, Drew Karpyshyn, and Casey Hudson; actors Jennifer Hale and Sam Witwer; video-game writer Walt Williams; and cosplayer Molly Chu. Without your stories—your honesty and generosity—this book would never have been written.

I owe an extra special thank-you to my editors at Boss Fight, Gabe Durham and Mike Williams, for having faith in this project long before I did. They were an endless source of wisdom, support, and patience as I worked to deliver the pages you hold in your hands. A debut author couldn't ask for a better pair of Jedi Masters. Thanks also to cover designer Cory Schmitz, layout designer Christopher Moyer, copyeditor Ryan Plummer, and proofreaders Joseph M. Owens and Nick Sweeney.

I'd also like to express my gratitude to former *Kill Screen* editors Chris Priestman and Will Partin, who gave me my start as a freelance journalist; to Miguel Lopez, Simon Cox, and John Davison, who showed me the ropes at *Rolling Stone*'s Glixel; and to Lucasfilm's Dan Brooks, who looked at my clips and decided to let me write for StarWars.com. I am incredibly lucky, and I take none of it for granted.

Another big thanks to Chris Baker and Janina Gavankar, for making invaluable introductions, and to Amanda Gonzalez, Danica Stanczak, and the rest of the PR folks at Lucasfilm and EA for their help and cooperation. Thank you to Shaun Duke, Rhian Stewart, Tyler Westhause, and everyone else who read and commented on various drafts and false starts along the way.

And, of course, all my love and appreciation to Ashleigh, my incredible wife. When I first began publishing professionally, she bought me a paperweight that said: "Do. Or do not. There is no try."

NOTES

The interviews that form the basis for this book were conducted between March 2017 and August 2018. Mike Gallo, Darragh O'Farrell, John Gallagher, Jennifer Hale, Sam Witwer, Walt Williams, and Molly Chu spoke to me on the phone. My interviews with James Ohlen and Drew Karpyshyn took place over Skype, and were arranged by EA. Haden Blackman and Simon Jeffery answered my questions via email.

Author's Note

George Lucas's comments on "the three worlds" of Star Wars come from Edward Douglas's interview with Lucas, "A Rare Sit-Down with Mr. George Lucas," published at ComingSoon. net on March 17, 2008: https://bit.ly/2GHN5Az

Ray Muzyka's confidence in *KotOR*'s place in the Star Wars canon was reported by Paul Marck in the *Edmonton Journal* article "Star Wars Tie-In Helps Make Firm a Force in Gaming," dated August 21, 2003.

The *ToyFare* poll, "May the Force Be with You," was posted on March 15, 2006, on WizardUniverse.com. An archived copy is here: https://bit.ly/2XvpdFE. The winner of this poll was actually Quinlan Vos, a Jedi who starred in various Dark Horse comics and then later appeared in the canon *Clones Wars* series, but Hasbro had already put a Quinlan figure into production. Darth Revan was the runner-up.

Winners of the Black Series were announced in a July 2, 2015 update to the fan poll "Vote for the Next Star Wars: The Black Series Six-Inch Figure," featured on the official Star Wars website: https://bit.ly/1RW9m8e.

Ray Muzyka's comments on player alignments were revealed in Joe Fielder's joint interview with Muzyka and Casey Hudson in the October 2003 issue of *Electronic Gaming Monthly*.

Muzyka's "two games in one box" comment is from "Alberta Adds to Star Wars Story," published in the newspaper the *Nanaimo Daily News* on August 16, 2003.

Drew Karpyshyn's statement that Revan "always belonged more to the fans" comes from a tweet posted December 30, 2016: https://bit.ly/2GGHLxr.

The figure of 270,000 Xbox units sold was announced by an official press release from LucasArts, "*Star Wars: Knights of the Old Republic* Posts Record Sales in First Two Weeks of Release," dated August 1, 2003. An archived copy is here: https://bit.ly/2SpdB3c.

James Ohlen's comments on the "big twist" are from "The BioWare Story," an episode in the *Magnum Opus Games* documentary series, first posted by Complex Originals on May 12, 2016: https://youtu.be/02YkHQuLTJU.

Aaron Boulding's review of *KotOR* on Xbox was published at IGN, July 14, 2003: https://bit.ly/2BST2qn.

Joe Fielder, Bryan Intihar, and Jennifer Tsao's review of *KotOR* on Xbox was published in *Electronic Gaming Monthly*'s September 2003 issue.

Green Light

Mary Bihr's comments on LucasArts's "survival mode" come from Rob Smith's *Rogue Leaders: The Story of LucasArts* (San Francisco: Chronicle Books, 2008), page 154.

Crackle and Hum

Mike Gallo's explanation of *KotOR*'s engine comes from GameSpot's "*Star Wars: Knights of the Old Republic* Q&A," published on November 5, 2002: https://bit.ly/2VeLmG5.

Mary Bihr's comment that "maybe archetypes weren't enough" comes from Frank Parisi and Daniel Erickson's *The Art and Making of Star Wars: The Old Republic* (San Francisco: Chronicle Books, 2011), page 16.

Binary System

The GameSpot reporter who noted that the combat between Jedi and Sith "resembled the final fight sequence in Episode I" was Amer Ajami. His "E3 2001 Hands-On: *Star Wars: Knights of the Old Republic*" was first published at GameSpot on May 19, 2001 (and republished on May 17, 2006): https://bit.ly/2GGGGWl. That same day, Ajami's "LucasArts Unveils BioWare RPG" noted BioWare's plans to release the game in late 2002: https://bit.ly/2EcJXcn.

Casey Hudson's comments on character-design pushback are from his interview with Joe Fielder in the October 2003 issue of *Electronic Gaming Monthly*.

The IGN writer who agreed *KotOR* footage looked "pretty damn nice" was Tal Blevins, in "Another Impressive Title from LucasArts at E3," published on May 22, 2001: https://bit.ly/2SofEV2.

Analog

John Barry and Roger Christian's term "used universe" is explained in J. W. Rinzler's foreword to *Cinema Alchemist*, by Roger Christian (London: Titan Books, 2016).

Casey Hudson's and Derek Watts's comments on character creation are from my article "BioWare and Capital Games on Bringing *KotOR* Fan Favorites Into *Galaxy of Heroes*," published at StarWars.com on July 13, 2018: https://bit.ly/2VhXMgu.

Information on Mission's character design comes from Jennifer Tsao's "20 Things You Didn't Know About *Knights of the Old Republic*," published in the November 2003 issue of *Electronic Gaming Monthly*.

VO

The PR team for Lucasfilm Games (Disney Interactive) couldn't officially confirm any numbers, but the database at MobyGames lists at least 78 Star Wars–related entries for Darragh O'Farrell from 1995 to 2017. Star Wars creator George Lucas has 114 such credits. Haden Blackman, who worked at LucasArts for 13 years, is credited on 47 Star Wars titles. When asked whether he's worked on more Star Wars games than anyone else in history, O'Farrell simply chuckled and said, "Probably."

Information on the extent of the game's script and dialogue is sourced from GameSpot's November 14, 2003 article "*Star Wars: Knights of the Old Republic* Q&A."

Tom Bissell's comments on Jennifer Hale are from his profile "Voicebox 360," published in *The New Yorker* on August 15, 2011: https://bit.ly/2XfhtY2.

Sleheyron

David Gaider's comments on Sleheyron's unsalvageable quest lines were posted November 1, 2003 in the BioWare Forums thread "Quick Character Question for the Devs." An archived copy may be found at http://archive.is/B4pTw.

Ray Muzyka's "39,000 bugs" comment is sourced from his interview with Joe Fielder in the October 2003 issue of *EGM*.

The Heart of the Force

Kieron Gillen's "I hate Star Wars" comment comes from his September 12, 2003 review of *KotOR* for Xbox at Eurogamer: https://bit.ly/2IxYfd6.

James Ohlen's comments on the benefits of owning original IPs come from Robert Purchese's "BioWare Had a Really Cool Idea for *Knights of the Old Republic II*," published at Eurogamer on December 12, 2017: https://bit.ly/2E7jLQk.

Mass Shadow

The value of $200 million assigned to *Star Wars: The Old Republic* comes from Alex Pham's "The Costliest Game of All Time?," published in the *Los Angeles Times* on January 20, 2012: https://lat.ms/2Nsr2OK.

Casey Hudson's comments on Mission and the magic of *KotOR*'s world come from my 2018 article "BioWare and Capital Games on Bringing *KotOR* Fan Favorites Into *Galaxy of Heroes*."

SPECIAL THANKS

For making our fourth season of books possible, Boss Fight Books would like to thank Cathy Durham, Edwin Locke, Nancy Magnusson-Durham, Ken Durham, Yoan Sebdoun-Manny, Tom Kennedy, Guillaume Mouton, Peter Smith, Mark Kuchler, Corey Losey, David Litke, James Terry, Patrick King, Nicole Kline, Seth Henriksen, Devin J. Kelly, Eric W. Wei, John Simms, Daniel Greenberg, Jennifer Durham-Fowler, Neil Pearson, Maxwell Neely-Cohen, Todd Hansberger, Chris Furniss, Jamie Perez, Joe Murray, and Mitchel Labonté.

ALSO FROM
BOSS FIGHT BOOKS